How to Talk to Anyone

Avoid Mistakes and Build Intense Conversations

(Build Stronger Communication and Make a Killer First Impression)

Thomas Calhoun

I0558267

Published By **Chris David**

Thomas Calhoun

How to Talk to Anyone: Avoid Mistakes and Build Intense Conversations (Build Stronger Communication and Make a Killer First Impression)

ISBN   978-1-998927-66-1

Legal & Disclaimer

The information contained in this book is not designed to replace or take the place of any form of medicine or professional medical advice. The information in this book has been provided for educational & entertainment purposes only.

The information contained in this book has been compiled from sources deemed reliable, and it is accurate to the best of the Author's knowledge; however, the Author cannot guarantee its accuracy and validity and cannot be held liable for any errors or omissions. Changes are periodically made to this book. You must consult your doctor or get professional medical advice before using any of the suggested remedies, techniques, or information in this book.

Table Of Contents

Chapter 1: Nine Principles For Conversing With Outsiders... 1

Chapter 2: 7 Things The Most Fascinating Individuals All Have Close To Normal..... 14

Chapter 3: The Nice Approach To Begin A Speak With An Outsider. 22

Chapter 4: Instructions On How To Make Casual Banter - Small Speak 36

Chapter 5: The Extensively Powerful Method To Preserve A Discussion Flowing: Tips And Advantages.............................. 54

Chapter 6: Eleven Methods For Remodeling Outsiders Into Companions 68

Chapter 7: Step Commands To Forestall An Easygoing Speak...................................... 77

Chapter 8: How To Master The Art Of Small Talk... 90

Chapter 9: How To Begin A Conversation With The Aid Of The Use Of Listening .. 108

Chapter 10: How To Keep A Conversation Going 123

Chapter 11: The Most Effective Method To Start A Conversation 162

Chapter 12: The Most Effective Method To Start A Conversation(Contd.) 174

Chapter 1: Nine Principles For Conversing With Outsiders

When you were a little one, did your mother and father assist you to recognise now not to talk with outsiders?

Such a massive range of individuals take keep of that advice lengthy after it quits being beneficial.

I loved very last inner with my family for a couple of months in the path of isolation. But given that we're out of lockdown, I'm making an funding greater electricity outdoor, I'm for the reason that my affect of outsiders has modified.

Studies display that even a quick discussion with a stranger will work to your kingdom of thoughts. Also, surely, this specifically consists of trivial casual discussion.

However, there are well and awful methods of making it show up. This isn't always a few factor we analyze at school - understandably -

bunches of people do now not have clean mind on a way to start.

So assuming which you're searching in advance to to take a stab at a few issue new and begin talking with outsiders on a greater normal foundation, right here are a few regulations for you.

1. Just converse with folks that

Want to talk with you.

This one need to be self-obvious, isn't that so?

Tragically, bunches of people bomb Stage One. They assume their responsibility is to steer the other man or woman that they want to have a talk.

That isn't always how this works! If someone is conveying clean messages that they may instead now not speak, you need to regard it. Even assuming you determined you understand better, no matter whether or not you are definitely exhausted or stressful to meet them.

Here is part of manners in which people might be advising you to ease off:

They're the usage of headphones/earphones

You cannot visually engage (making eye touch) with them or they're tenaciously taking a gander at some thing one-of-a-type (or keeping their eyes near, assuming that could be a public adventure scenario)

Their non-verbal communique (frame language) is close off: palms crossed, hands stowed away

I likewise set off wariness to communicate with individuals who look furious, demanding, depleted, or anyhow now not inside the mind-set for a go to. Focus on the ones signs and symptoms. Odds are they really want to be left by myself.

Then all over again, you can make any person's shitty day highly higher - quite in all likelihood speakme with you may help for the cause that it's less complicated to consider in outsiders.

On the off hazard which you study someone crying, provide them a tissue and backpedal assuming they display no hobby in speaking with you. In any case, assuming you lay out a watch-to-eye connection and check that talk is gladly acquired, provide grace and inquire as to whether there can be something you can do.

2. There are not any all-inclusive requirements...

However, that does not recommend there are no requirements by way of manner of using any stretch of the creativeness. Apologies, I want it have been sincerely clean.

There are a big range of implicit assumptions concerning how discussions amongst outsiders must pass down. Many of these rely on elements which is probably from your manage, just like improvement in years, orientation, tradition, religion, class, and so forth. The behavior furthermore is based upon the state, metropolis, and, quite, the neighborhood you are in.

The setting is essential. For instance, it could thoroughly be superb to begin a dialogue in a vivid, swarmed park, however that identical park is surely not a suitable spot for a go to within the middle of the night.

So how might you finalize whether or not or no longer or not it's miles OK to start speaking with an intruder?

It's all the manner all of the manner down to thriller and karma. You need to invest some energy in seeing what others are doing and observe their model. Here and there, it's miles proper to be attempting and start up a dialogue irrespective of whether or not you do not understand it suits the manners - however as an opportunity once more, follow Stage One, and by no means press the hassle on the off chance that it appears your technique isn't desired.

3. Keep your non-verbal verbal exchange open and awesome.

Remain open to signals, and moreover make sure you are conveying the right messages decrease lower again.

Keep your frame free, collectively in conjunction with your fingers thru your factors and your hands-on show. Make an attempt now not to droop or twist in on your self. A grin merits 1,000 terms, however, your veil may be concealing it these days - so try to provide eye-to-eye connection, all matters being equal. However, strive not to gaze. Specialists say that suitable eye contact lasts 4-5 seconds, and going over that throws off every person's vibe.

You ought to likewise regard the outsider's very very personal space. Don't swarm them, nook them, or loom over them. Social distancing makes this extra large than any time in modern-day reminiscence, however the equal antique holds in latest. According to experts, 4 toes is the lowest courteous distance for outsiders within the US, but, another time, this is based totally upon your way of existence and considered one of a kind elements.

4. Regularly start with a" howdy" or " howdy."

Simply say good day or hello.

You do not want to astonish them from the primary word. Assuming you attempt, you'll in all likelihood offer a few element humiliating. Begin honest, make proper pals or gesture. Grinning is probably the primary concept but it usually isn't always just sufficient to begin a talk

.

Your unique day will likewise determine the diploma of conference among you and the opportunity character. "Hello" is ok for public journey, "thrilled to meet you" is probably the most perfect choice at a assembly.

I apprehend this detail can enjoy off-kilter, but assuming you're an English speaker, you could keep in mind yourself lucky - essentially, you do not need to determine out Vous/tu qualifications!

Five. Ask questions.

Whenever you've got welcomed the opportunity individual, pose an inquiry. Once greater, it shouldn't be some problem stunning. "How are you?" can turn out incredible, or maybe "I surprise if it'll rain yet again?"

Recall that no longer something lousy can honestly be said approximately little communicate. It makes everything drift without issue in the discussion and also you do no longer want to paintings up your mind.

When the talk begins rolling, you can pose inquiries that require longer solutions - it's miles best to choose open-ended questions and live far from ones that may be replied to in a single phrase.

However, I start little. On the off chance that the opposite person is not keen on chipping in records or posing inquiries consequently, this communicate wasn't intended to be.

6. Be careful with praises.

Alongside questions, praises are an regular communique starter. Yet, this is dubious terrain. A few commendations appear to be contemptible. They can reason it to seem as no matter the truth that you are promoting some issue or seeking out a telephone amount.

A first rate important rule: in no way praise a stranger's actual capabilities. Stick to clothes, footwear, frills, or some detail that the individual is doing. Hair is a borderline case - if any man or woman has an tough, pleasant haircut, a commendation might also additionally need to land properly, but, it is by way of using the usage of and huge higher now not to raise a few element related with individual grooming

Praising any individual's baby is exciting as nicely and is based totally upon the manner of existence and placing. Is the child mature enough to get you? Do you have were given a little one with you as well? Once greater, it's miles higher no longer to commend the children's actual highlights, no matter the fact that pronouncing a little one is lovable will in trendy be OK.

(Some uplifting information for you - pets are commonly notable to commend.)

7. Settle on some thing nicely well worth agreeing on.

You've loosened topics up, and presently it is the right time to get the communicate moving. What do you simply communicate?

The response is that you need to triangulate. Find a few component which you and the outsider share almost talking, and afterward communicate approximately that.

Try no longer to talk about the alternative person straightforwardly, and do no longer talk yourself at the identical time both. All things taken into consideration, speak about a capability commonplace come across. Has the weather conditions been wild presently? Is this running route higher compared to a few other nearby? Do you've got got a (powerful) assessment on the dental expert you're every going to see? Of direction, bring that up.

Yet all over again pets are lifelines for the reason that, in such a case that you and the outsider each very non-public pets, you could speak it proper away.

Eight. Make it clean you're focusing.

After the triangulation, you may flow on to more profound subjects - conceivably.

To make the dialogue certainly interesting, you actually need to offer close interest and ask some subsequent inquiries.

You will not commonly get the specific interplay you're looking for.Some element it is able to, some of the time, the opposite man or woman will open established upon you. You may additionally take a look at something critical with a view to alternate your thoughts-set. Simply maintain a receptive outlook and focus nearer on them than on yourself.

Then once more, you cannot expect truthfulness and transparency without giving some thing as a trade-off. So take a stab at being sincere along side your outsider - you could unburden your self of some thing that has been annoying you for a while..

9. Advice isn't desired a hundred% of the time.

Like commendations, steering may be a -sided deal. You might likely as an opportunity not look like belittling or annoying.

Before you provide exhortation, discover if it's miles a few aspect that the character simply doesn't comprehend however. "Hey, the following avenue is close down, you may no longer have the selection to undergo!" is tremendous endorse. "I may in no way buy that, it's miles brimming with sugar." is sincerely you being a meddling butt sphincter.

This is going twofold for unsolicited nurturing endorse. Except if it's miles a catastrophe (for example, each person in truth did not see that their infant strayed), sincerely say not some thing. They've possibly heard the whole lot formerly.

You can really loosen up - you can get better at this!

Assuming you are feeling debilitated after this Advice, sit down again and loosen up. Concurring with the arena's the usage of draw near on speakme with outsiders, you for the most detail want to pay interest, assignment yourself, and permit your sympathy expand.

What's more, on the off hazard which you're not but prepared to speak with outsiders, there may be some detail you may do in education. Learn a way to be an interesting individual and those will speedy start firing up discussions with you.

Chapter 2: 7 Things The Most Fascinating Individuals All Have Close To Normal

1) First, Don't be silly

Sometimes, the excellent offense is a first-rate safety. See it much like the Hippocratic Vow of conversations: Do Not harm.

We are in famous horrendous at acknowledging whilst we bore others due to the fact, virtually, we as an entire suspect we're sincerely entrancing.

The #1 tip for in no way boring all people: Be quick, be splendid.

Assuming which you're typically forthright and continue to be upbeat, it's miles especially tough for absolutely everyone in price you for being a negative industrial business enterprise commercial enterprise agency.

Yet, sometimes you certainly do have to speak specifically longer to make certain subjects don't get unnatural.

The Craft of Humanized Conversation gives one greater fantastic tip: Is in truth each person asking you approximately what you are speaking approximately?

If it simply is now not, probable now's the proper time to quit the story or pose the alternative man or woman an inquiry.

2) The Most Captivating Individuals Are Regularly Great listeners

Intriguing individuals can be exquisite, however, it could likewise regress into popularity maneuvering, need to experience advanced, and jealousy.

Individuals love to speak about themselves and there can be a shortage of desirable listeners.

Allow the opportunity person to talk. It gives their mind as heaps delight as food or coins:

Discussing ourselves-whether or not in an character communicate or via net-primarily based media places like Facebook and

Twitter-units off a comparable vibe of pleasure inside the thoughts as food or cash...

You can set up an extremely good connection via pronouncing rather little. Ironically, people we just like the most often say the least.

Three) Talk About The Other Individual's Inclinations

This is straight away from an professional Socialist and if you're no longer that socially professional, that is greater or a fantastic deal tons much less direct.

Why struggle to consider what most human beings can also locate conventionally captivating?

Ask people what they were as much as or what their component hobbies are (hobbies). Then, at that thing, speak approximately that. You're currently 80% of the manner there.

On the off threat which you comprehend about the project, the likeness will bond you.

On the off chance which you do now not, request that they make clean and be an superb listener as they speak about a few issue they love.

Four) Have Three Great Stories

Jokesters do not definitely speak about a few thing at the same time as they're within the the front of an target market. They have their demonstration practiced.

You do no longer truly run into a bit interview and get out anything this is at the leading fringe of your mind.

Continuously have 3 incredible stories nearby that dependably engage, light up, or lock in.

One extra tip from an professional: People are with the aid of and huge keener on anecdotes approximately humans rather than topics.

Show, tattle, and reality television are fruitful on purpose. We as an entire observe the human way of behaving captivatingly.

Then again, the extremely good majority may want to as an possibility now not love to discover approximately the skills of your new iphone.

5) Remember aura

It's no longer about the words. Certain humans are connecting, but, assuming what they said have come to be translated, it would be unimpressive.

While you are speaking emotionally, the words just file 7% of what receives conveyed. Seven percentage!.

Voice tone and non-verbal verbal exchange are undeniably extra significant.

One often referred to investigate positioned that of all of the information surpassed right now to a person else whilst we offer a few element enthusiastic (not academic), really 7% is contained in the actual importance of the terms we use.

Snicker. Grin. Be enthusiastic. Signal. Tweak your voice. Don't definitely perspire the phrases.

6) Be Somewhere Fascinating

Got a say in wherein you will be at, likewise with a date or meeting?

Pick somewhere animating. Setting topics.

As a extremely-present day rule, we're junky approximately acknowledging wherein our sentiments are coming from.

Research shows satisfaction from any deliver is frequently connected with the individual you are with - regardless of whether or no longer they're no longer the cause for it.

For what motive in all truth do individuals take a look at artists so captivating? The tune and the employer animate feelings - and we instinctively companion humans with the band.

For what cause does this get up? Experts determine it could have something to do with "misattribution of feelings": "In some times, we have a unethical and we haven't any idea in which it is coming from, so we form of stick it on a few component that appears to be affordable." At the save you of the day, your overwhelming tendencies in the direction of the tune should make you take delivery of as actual with you're having overwhelming tendencies inside the path of the lead vocalist.

7) And In particular: live A Fascinating Life

Do you Recall the priority remember: If you want to be a knight, maintain on like a knight.

If you do no longer peruse, watch and contemplate non-specific matters, conventional topics are a great deal much less willing to emerge from your mouth.

This ought to not be costly or difficult. Hang out greater frequently with the most charming human beings you realise.

The companions you invest strength with dramatically have an impact on your conduct - whether or now not you need it or now not.

The Life span Undertaking, which taken into consideration over a thousand people from kids to no prevent had this to mention:

The gatherings you partner with frequently determine the kind of individual you turn out to be.

In The Start-up of You, specialists speak about how the maximum great manner to art work on precise traits in yourself is to invest energy with those who within the mean time are similar to that.

The awesome and most dependable approach for seeming charming is to stay an interesting life.

Chapter 3: The Nice Approach To Begin A Speak With An Outsider.

Through the direction of your artwork, you are likely going to meet a few new people, every outside and inside your affiliation. Knowing the way to start discussions with outsiders is a treasured tool as you discover new expert connections. Layout and an person rundown of capability ice breakers that will help you with winning on this location. In this ebook, we offer mind and times of compelling strategies of beginning a communicate with an intruder.

Starting a massive talk with an intruder can sense off-kilter and harrowing from the start. Whether you are informed at starting discussions or battle with making casual verbal exchange, understanding how and in which to begin is a huge ability. Survey those way for starting a discussion with an intruder:

Be exceptional: Go into the communicate with an inspirational attitude. Keep up with turning into non-verbal verbal exchange to depict your electricity, which includes grinning and uncrossing your fingers.

Take a profound breath: Take a development of entire breaths before beginning the communicate. This will help with easing returned your pulse and help with assuaging any anxiety.

Stay aware of the outsider's time: If the outsider appears occupied or focused, have a pass at keeping your communicate quick.

20 methods for starting a communicate with an outsider

Review and have a study the ones 20 ice breakers that will help you with feeling greater excellent at the same time as transferring in the direction of an interloper:

1. Accumulate facts

One feasible method for beginning a communicate with an intruder is to pose them a query or a improvement of inquiries. Contingent upon the scenario, you can get some records about the climate, what they're having for lunch or about a common expert obligation. Think approximately this model:

Example: "Do you understand whether or no longer the company president will deal with us eventually of the initial meeting?"

Give care to their response and ponder different associated questions or feedback you may make to make all of the difference for the discussion.

2. Praise the outsider

One greater approach for starting a talk with some different person is to reward them. This method almost constantly activates a cute verbal exchange about the thing or thing you've got endorsed. Think approximately this version:

Example: "I like your briefcase."

To make all the difference for this speak, have a flow into at the usage of some next inquiries, for example, wherein they supplied the briefcase and on the off risk that it's miles to be had in numerous solar sun shades.

3. Raise a common state of affairs

Make Use of your environmental elements to help you lay out a talk with an interloper. For instance, assuming that you are going to an corporation gathering, ask the man or woman near you at a studio their opinion on the occasion. Assuming which you're snatching lunch, call hobby to the one which you love dish to the man or woman close to you in line. Here is some other version:

Example: "Do you decide inside the shape? I observed your automobile packed near mine the day prior to this."

4. Introduce your self

An introduction is a smooth technique to beginning a discussion with an intruder. It's particularly powerful assuming there might be no one in every of a type smooth ice breakers to rely upon. Here is a model:

Example: "Hi, I'm Andrew. I certainly moved in right here and I needed to acquaint myself with anyone inside the branch."

Without a doubt, the individual you are assembly will percent their call and particular facts approximately their state of affairs with you, prompting a comfortable dialogue.

5. Ask open-ended inquiries (questions)

One more exceptional method for starting a speak with an intruder is to pose open-ended inquiries. This device works brilliant at the identical time as you are going on a commonplace event and may get some facts about the opportunity man or woman's perception. For instance:

Example: "I certainly have in no way been to such an interesting workshop. What approximately you?"

By and huge, the alternative birthday party have to solution with their sentiments or tales approximately fantastic conferences they have got joined in, introducing extra conversational elements for you.

6. Keep conscious-to-date on present day-day tendencies

Recent inclinations are incredible ice breakers. It's prudent to reference non-political sports if you and the stranger have contrasting views. Consider elements like a network party, or get some data approximately some distinctive ebook or as of past due introduced film. Here is a model:

Example: "Did you spot the every year Occasion Celebration starts offevolved offevolved one week from now? I usually recognize on foot round and seeing the adornments."

7. Propose to help

Assuming which you see an intruder struggling with with an assignment, providing to help them is an super technique for starting a dialogue. Contingent upon the area and putting of the collaboration, you could employ a model like this:

Example: "Let me bring that container for you! Are you new to the building?"

8. Share an interesting reality

This approach is first-class applied at the equal time as you are in a place or state of affairs in which your thrilling reality straightforwardly relates. When applied fittingly, this method may be profoundly compelling for drawing in a few different man or woman right into a talk. Here is a model:

Example: "Did you recognize that absolutely, lifts are the most regular approach for voyaging?"

Nine. Request their standpoint

Don't forget asking a stranger for his or her component of view to start a communicate.

This is an exceptional technique on the off hazard which you're out elsewhere or searching out pens to your agency's stock storeroom. This is an example of the manner to make use of this device:

Example: "Which of these highlighters do you need wonderful? I typically make use of these yellow ones, but the wax ones look genuinely captivating!"

10. Request lunch steering

One prevailing gadget for beginning a speak with an intruder is to get a few statistics approximately their cherished lunch place. This is mainly beneficial on the off threat which you're in a lift or sitting tight for a taxi or public transportation as it very well may be a fast communicate.

Example: "Where do you like to eat round here?

I in preferred exercising session of the Fifth Road administrative center, so I'm inexperienced with this area of town."

The more weird will in all likelihood impart their cherished eating places to you, and they could even welcome you to go together with them for lunch.

Eleven. Remark on a viral video

Viral recordings are a likely conversational tool. Many human beings watch recordings of their excursion or seize wind of them from their companions or companions. Assuming you employ this device, guarantee the video you look at is paintings-suitable. Here is a version:

Example: "Have you visible the video of the kid nodding off within the frozen yogurt bowl?"

Ideally, this will activate a communicate approximately different charming recordings or mainstream society topics.

12. Be smooth

Anywhere, the quality way to begin a speak is to be on the spot approximately the detail you are looking for or need. For instance, on the off danger that you're misplaced, request bearings. To have lunch with every other man or woman, specific that plainly. Here is any other version:

Example: "Today is my first day, and I don't have any concept in which to move for lunch. Would you word any problems assuming I went at the side of you?"

13. Request help

Asking for help is a prevailing technique for starting a dialogue. Contingent upon the situation, you will possibly have to ask a selected character in choice to every body close by for assist. Think about this version:

Example: "I even have no longer labored out of this place of job previously, so I do not understand approximately the way this skills. Would you notice any troubles with assisting me?"

14. Talk approximately normal pastimes

In high-quality occurrences, it very well can be smooth you proportion an interest with an interloper. Use the signal you consider a method planning stage for the speak:

Example: "I see you likewise test our nearby b-ball organization. I nowadays went to a recreation the week in advance than! Have you been to any video video games this month?"

15. Offer a smart statement

One extra technique for beginning a communicate with an outsider is to declaration at the state of affairs in which you music down your self. This approach works top notch whilst there is a particular component to statement on, for instance:

Example: "I see you likewise simply like to make use of the handset in area of a headset."

This form of declaration allows outsiders to percentage their non-public sentiments concerning the hassle.

Sixteen. Notice a commonplace characteristic

Utilize this method at the same time as you're fantastic you and the extra exciting provide a normal characteristic. Making communicate about a commonplace characteristic is frequently an outstanding method for shaping a 2nd affiliation. Think about this version:

Example: "I saw you recommended it along side your left hand - I'm a lefty, as nicely!"

Whenever novel attributes are worried, the big majority apprehend analyzing the association.

17. Pose an inquiry approximately their enjoy

Getting some information approximately their revel in is an expert and inviting method for beginning a dialogue. Think about this version:

Example: "Welcome to the organization! Where had been you in advance than you went collectively with us right right right here?"

18. Request steering

Look for steering from a stranger for beginning a dialogue. In a high-quality global, hold the guidance you ask proficient and linked collectively with your cutting-edge-day situation. Think about this version:

Example: "I'm now not high-quality which format I need to use for my display. Would you notice any troubles with investigating and imparting me a few steerage?"

19. Remark on a not unusual motion

Another open door is to announcement on a not unusual movement or hobby assuming that it's miles self-obvious. For example, you could see a stranger sporting a pin from the one that you love show scene or an man or woman perusing a e-book you love in the entryway of your structure. Think about this version:

Example: "I see you have got been analyzing whilst we had been given off the tram. I certainly completed that e-book every week in the past! Is it actual which you are loving it?"

20. Make a quip

Another gadget you could utilize for starting a dialogue with an intruder is to guide them to a wisecrack. This is exceptional completed if the comedian tale applies to the condition in which you land up with the outsider. For instance:

Example: "You realize what can simply make your Friday a great deal less first-rate? Recollecting that it's just Thursday."

Chapter 4: Instructions On How To Make Casual Banter - Small Speak

On the off hazard which you occasionally visit networking events or get-togethers, you in all likelihood participate in casual banter with new people you meet. However informal dialogue begins offevolved as a light speak, it is able to set out open doors for reliable, huge discussions. Auditing the technique for the manner to make casual banter will assist you to all of the greater take part in a speak at your subsequent get-collectively.

In this ebook, we examine what informal verbal exchange is, how you can make casual chit chat, and some more tips that will help you with doing such greater in reality.

What is casual banter?

Casual chit chat is a informal kind of debate this is now and again implemented among individuals who don't know each other properly fashionable, as an example, in the course of networking or get-togethers. Casual chitchat is furthermore a door to a greater pinnacle-to-the-bottom talk, a manner for severa gatherings to look similarly into what they percent practically speakme until they track down a subject of commonplace hobby.

Step with the resource of step commands to make informal conversation.

The following are six levels you can contain to definitely make casual communicate and begin discussions in any state of affairs:

1. Show real hobby

The preliminary step to honestly making casual conversation is to show genuine hobby inside the individual with whom you're talking. See it as a hazard to in fact get to recognize the man or woman you are talking with and gain from them. Remember on the identical time as you start speaking that each discussion gives any other open door. The communicate must bring about each extraordinary fellowship or they may truly exchange into a few other client.

2. Utilize open-finished questions

A super many people like to speak approximately themselves and factors that they understand about. Empower more in-intensity responses by way of posing open-ended questions. One approach is to start a speak with a sincere inquiry and in some time circle once more to open-ended ones.

For example, you could start by the use of asking in which any man or woman is from and in a while get some facts about that vicinity for fantastic what their vintage network grow to be like. Assuming you're at a Networking event and lead via manner of asking someone how they make ends meet, you may have a look at up through asking them how they got here to be in that place.

3. Practice undivided attention

To frame the awesome association with the opportunity character at the same time as making informal discussion, exercising undivided interest. Undivided attention-active listening is a specialized method that consists of deliberately focusing on the phrases that the speaker is the usage of

Not surely will the opportunity individual study how drawn in you're in the dialogue, yet you can likewise see that because it's more sincere to invite applicable next inquiries. You'll likewise be positive to appearance and keep in mind key subtleties that you can get some records about later inside the communicate.

To be a greater attentive individual - an active listener, strive making visible connections sort of 60% of the time whilst the alternative man or woman is talking. Intermittently nod your head to truely display which you're tuning in and continue to be honestly present and loose. At the point at the equal time because the speaker stops, pose inquiries to offer an motive for what they are speaking about.

4. Utilize the 20-2nd rule

Be privy to how masses time you're speaking. Whenever you have got been speaking for round 20 seconds, strive to finish your contemplations. You have to be finished talking on the same time as you arrive on the 40-2nd mark. Consider this preferred a fixed of traffic indicators. For the number one 20-second imprint, you have were given the bypass-beforehand to speak. Whenever you arrive at 20 seconds, the slight adjustments to yellow and whilst you get to 40 seconds, the moderate is pink, and now's the right time to permit the opposite individual to speak.

Five. Be aware of your non-verbal verbal exchange

Your non-verbal communique signs and symptoms and signs and symptoms and signs like earnest gesturing, eye-to-eye connection, and inclining bring to the stranger which you are eager on what they want to say. Ensure which you're grinning while right, are focusing, and function your arms uncrossed.

6. Decisively plan your exit

Whenever you've got arrived on the stop of your talk, it is able to help with having a easy and regular stop organized. You can clearly allow them to apprehend that it become fantastic accumulating them and in some time reference something you pointed out at a few degree in the speak. For example, assuming you meet a person who's searching for a brand new function, you may desire them karma with their pursuit of employment. To maintain in contact and in addition foster the connection, you may welcome them to advantage you on the off chance that there can be some detail you may do to help with their hunt.

Ways to make informal banter

Beneath are some guidelines to don't forget at the same time as you are making informal banter:

★   Have the right mentality.

It's important to have the proper outlook earlier than you leave for a get-together in which you could make casual banter. To do that, remind yourself why you are going and what you are anticipating escaping the event.

Conclude who you want to fulfill ahead of time:

Assuming that there's a dispensed rundown of individuals, recall taking a gander on the rundown and concluding who you would probably want to associate with earlier of time. This can help you with digging into the event and installation more than one inquiries to use to kick the dialogue off.

★ Listen extra than you talk

The most first-class way to transform informal dialogue right into a noteworthy speak is to really be privy to what the opposite individual is speaking about and urge them to talk extra. Attempt to take a look at a factor that the opposite man or woman is eager on and urge them to teach you extra. If they pose you an inquiry, percent a few issue individual about your self and urge them to draw in with you similarly.

★   Request steerage

A first-rate many people like being requested guidance from, particularly at the off chance that it is a part they may be profoundly familiar with. Think of asking for exhortation to kick a discussion off

★   Try no longer to make use of your phone

Studies display that the presence of a phone can smash a communicate. Leave your telephone for your sack or pocket and oppose the impulse to position it at the table close to you. On the off chance which you are anticipating a large message, allow the opposite character recognize earlier of time and make an apology before going after your mobile phone.

★   Have questions organized

Beginning a communicate with another man or woman may be a assignment. Have inquiries as a number one trouble that you could use to start discussions with any man or woman you don't have the foggiest idea. Questions like, "how could you understand [name]" or "how may want to you discover this occasion" may be an top notch spot to start.

★   Assume a enjoy of possession with assembly human beings

Rather than trusting that any character will drift in the direction of you, be the person to make right buddies first. The greater times you method some different character, the greater agreeable you may develop into.

7 English Casual banter ideas for Beginning Cordial Discussions.

1. Presentations / Introducing your self

Before you may get to apprehend a person, it's miles truely smart to offer your self.

You can acquaint yourself with every person you do not realize, or to remind all people you've got met earlier than who have to have did not recollect you. While you are presenting your self, you can upload a tad of facts like in which you to start with met, for excessive great you do. You would possibly probable comprise your English studying as an ice breaker.

Models:

"Good day! We generally have coffee simultaneously but we have got in no way spoken. I pass via [Your Name]."

"Hi, how's it setting with you? I am [Your Name]. I'm in reality gaining knowledge of English so kindly permit me apprehend as to whether or not or now not I make any mistakes."

"Hey, Angela. You probable may not recall me, but we met at Tom's Christmas party remaining three hundred and sixty five days. I'm [Your Name]."

2. General Themes (Universal subjects)

General problems may be shared thru nearly simply anyone.

Things just like the weather, contemporary-day data, sports activities sports activities, and leisure are normally no-trouble ice breakers, especially at the same time as you're addressing a meeting regardless of whether or not or no longer one individual truely watches sports activities sports sports, any other character within the collecting can also.

Albeit the ones issues are discussed through some of people, tremendous people likely might not be lovers of sports activities activities activities, or in all likelihood may not observe enjoyment facts, so if you can, try and fit human beings' tendencies to the concern you select. For instance, on the off danger that you've heard them discussing extraordinary evaluations in advance than, you can strive to speak about a report from these days.

Models:

"Did you watch the Oscars final week? I can't absolutely take shipping of that Leonardo dicaprio, at last, won one!"

"This weather circumstance is insane! Yesterday become bloodless and in recent times I got here in with an open coat. I accept as genuine with it remains warm temperature, do not you?"

"That b-ball undertaking the previous day had me stuck to my seat. Wasn't that an awesome keep at the surrender?"

Three. The Day

If you do no longer recognize approximately what subject matter to talk approximately or do not have some component captivating to say, you may honestly get a few information approximately their day, or you could communicate yours.

For example, you may ask them:

How have become your day? / How did your day move?

How have you ever been feeling nowadays?

What have you ever ever been thus far?

Has some aspect energized befell in recent times?

What are you getting geared up for after artwork?

Is it actual or now not which you are doing some factor amusing after paintings?

You can likewise percentage facts approximately your day and the way you're doing, however, try to keep a harmony among speakme and tuning in, so you every get to speak a similar sum (and you're no longer truly discussing yourself the complete time).

Regardless of whether or not the character appears as even though they've been having an lousy day, you can make it more wonderful in reality with the aid of the use of way of creating a informal dialogue! Try not to pose excessively personal inquiries, and on 2nd belief offer some best inspirational statements.

Models:

"Hello. You appear as despite the fact that you are having an ugly day. I preference it receives higher for you."

"Good day! I went putting in camp on Saturday, and obviously, it rained all day. Was your surrender of the week any better?"

"The day is type of finished! Do you have got were given were given any charming plans for the night time time?"

Four. The Workplace

A few discussions are just appropriate for the paintings surroundings.

Remain even lots less non-public at art work than in extra easygoing spots, and keep away from meddling (discussing others who are absent)! All topics considered, you may speak the day, an drawing near party or assembly, or get a few data about the individual's paintings.

Models:

"Hey, Tom. How can topics bypass over on the IT department these days?"

"Hello. I'm sincerely looking forward to the birthday celebration after artwork these days. I concentrate Pam added her renowned carrot cake!"

"What a bustling day. This have to be the number one time I are becoming up from my seat all day. Were you occupied too?"

Five. Perceptions/observations

The absolute first-class casual banter is about in which you and your speak associate are placed.

It's a few element you each have in commonplace, so there may be no scenario that they may not understand what you are speakme about. Glance round and tune down some detail to assertion on, or take a gander at your associate and music down some thing great to commend them on. Nothing encourages humans more than an real commendation!

Models:

"I love your footwear, they really in shape your outfit."

"Did you notice? They at lengthy remaining regular the light in the living room. It's been damaged for close to 30 days!"

"Hello Pam, your treats the previous middle of the night were flavorful! Much thanks to you for making them for the birthday party."

6. Normal Interests

When you have a few aspect almost identical along with your speaking companion, it implies you've got some detail to speak about. Track down a shared interest (an hobby you each understand) or enjoyment hobby, and you could have a few component to speak approximately.

Remember that English audio device seldom in truth offer the signal "enjoyment interest," so inquiring "What are your issue interests?" sounds uncommon and unnatural. Take a stab at posing questions alternatively, based totally on observations.

Models:

"My cousin referenced you the previous evening. I did not recognize you knew her! Where did you meet?"

"I observed your cap has a Yankees brand. Do you appreciably love baseball as properly?"

"I had a go at baking treats like yours this evening; they got here out terrible. How do you are making them so first rate?"

7. Questions

You ought to have visible at this factor that the more a part of those casual communique fashions stocks some element for all intents and purposes: They ask questions. A tremendous technique for beginning a dialogue is to say some element, then, at that point, pose an inquiry. It holds the dialogue from terminating in your commentary (and making topics a good buy extra bizarre!).

While asking questions, listen as heaps as you speak, and do now not get excessively personal together at the side of your inquiries. Also, make certain to hold matters excessive amazing!

Models:

"Hello, I heard you have been considering getting a few other cat. Did you find out one?"

"i've been seeking to invite you this for some time: how lengthy have you ever been running right here?"

"Your hair commonly appears lovely. What hair cream do you employ?"

Whenever you are with anyone and no individual is speaking, you realize what to do!

Chapter 5: The Extensively Powerful Method To Preserve A Discussion Flowing: Tips And Advantages

Discussion is a fundamental piece of regular each day lifestyles that affects a person's functionality to deliver contemplations and thoughts. It's vital to look a way to push a talk alongside as it allows you to make super institutions with others and bring your necessities. By know-how a way to hold a speak, you could enhance as a conversationalist for your private and expert life.

In this bankruptcy, we observe why it's miles critical to have incredible speak abilties, audit key blessings of having the selection to hold a speak, provide tips to shifting a communicate alongside and bear in mind a rundown of steps for a way to make a big distinction for a talk.

What are talk talents and for what purpose would probably they may be pronouncing they're vast?

Discussion abilties are relational features that permit human beings to speak approximately efficaciously with others. Discussion abilities encompass undivided hobby, language usage, compassion, and narrating. It is essential to have extraordinary talk talents considering the reality that it's miles able that will help you with expertly introducing your self at artwork. The following are more than one more instances of why first-rate communicate capabilities are remarkable:

★   Lays out substantial professional establishments

By using great talk skills, you could purpose others to experience esteemed. It furthermore empowers you to foster the communicate similarly to get extra familiar with each exceptional and your professional advantages.

★   Empowers commonplace association

If you understand how to banter with others and retain with discussions, you could help the alternative man or woman with getting your perspectives and locating out approximately theirs as well. By data each notable, you have got a advanced possibility of preserving up with great correspondence and functioning admirably collectively.

★ Assists you with articulating your mind

Knowing a way to speak with others lets in you to percentage your worries and mind expressively. This famous your extraordinary capability and assists you with obtaining assist for numerous sports or undertakings.

Advantages of maintaining a speak

In the right placing, maintaining a talk will assist you to in an series of strategies. The following are multiple instances of while you may benefit from keeping a talk:

★ During new employee screenings

While assembly for an interview, longer meetings would possibly possibly show which you have a advanced opportunity of pushing in advance with a employer. Your capability to maintain a communicate with a recruiting administrator by using using posing awesome inquiries, making casual communication, and giving in-depth responses can help them with diving more deeply into your competencies and it indicates that you care about the scenario being referred to.

★ During structures control events

Networking occasions are terrific methods for assembly one-of-a-type experts and predicted companies. On the off chance that you can hold a speak with any other professional, you may lay out a long-haul Networking association that could activate destiny positions or partnerships.

★ During client gatherings

For the folks who art work in gives and purchaser individuals of the family, having the choice to hold a talk influences your potential to get new customers and restore consumer contracts. This is because you recognize a manner to interface with others, cause them to revel in esteemed, and communicate approximately topics exhaustively.

★ During group duties

Keeping up with discussions on the same time as operating with a gathering of collaborators guarantees that you understand your desires each and get your jobs and paintings within the route of a comparable goal. It can likewise assist you and your colleagues with studying every brilliant and manual your organization's standard overall performance degrees.

Ways to preserve a talk

Here are a few recommendations that will help you with preserving a speak and getting large gestures:

★ Work on retaining up with discussions to your private existence

The outstanding technique for keeping a talk is to rehearse till you get cushty talking to others. You can rehearse with a associate or loved one, or you may rehearse with outsiders at the identical time as at the store or a neighborhood region event. By growing your ordinary fashion of familiarity and finding out about the types of inquiries human beings solution, you can foster accommodating strategies to keep up with discussions.

★ Utilize undivided hobby

Undivided hobby- lively listening is the interaction via manner of way of which you skip your emphasis and hobby without delay to the speaker. This carries visually connecting, gesturing, and making short verbal motions. If an man or woman appears like you are genuinely intrigued via using way of what they need to say, they will be extra able to amplify on the thing and hold talking with you.

Try not to talk truely to fill the quietness in some unspecified time in the future of pauses.

While speakme to others, specifically the ones you do now not understand well, a quiet second or brief remove could cause you to enjoy devoted to speakme. Nonetheless,

★ Know even as to end the communicate

Each communicate has an endpoint, and a few give up greater rapidly than others. This could no longer imply you probably did no longer have a charming discussion with them, it definitely implies you have got talked about all that you may have the ability. By perusing the opportunity person's non-verbal conversation, you can survey whether or not they will be organized to maintain on from the communicate. Close via way of pronouncing way to them for his or her time and you may give them your contact statistics if vital.

The simplest approach to keep up a dialogue Survey those way to determine a way to make all of the difference for a speak:

1. Ask follow-up inquiries

Follow-up questions are those which you ask after the underlying inquiry about problems that the speaker will increase of their response. This is an amazing approach for pushing a speak along, and it suggests your interest in what the person holds to mention. Asking brilliant subsequent inquiries expects you to pay interest mindfully and endure in mind little subtleties.

For instance:

"How did you get into digital marketing?"

"I took an intro to digital advertising course in school and It involved me."

"That is awesome. So wherein did you move to high school?"

2. Incorporate a tale or model with questions that consist of a 'advantageous' or 'no' response

Expounding on answers that could some way or every different be "sure" or "no" permits you the opportunity to stretch the talk and rouse observe-up inquiries from the audience.

For example;

Assuming every person inquires as to whether you are from the region, you can provide some factor like this:

"No, I'm from Chicago, Illinois, but, this warmth weather situation is marking me to reexamine my selections. Where are you from?"

3. Praise the alternative character

On the off chance which you do now not know what to say right now, praise the person's hairdo, garments, or one among their achievements approximately. This assists you with pushing the dialogue alongside as it permits the opposite individual to talk greater about a issue, and it allows you to pose extra inquiries.

The following are or three one-of-a-type techniques you could do that:

"Your speech changed into so rousing. How did you enhance at public talking?"

"I love your Maryland cap. Is it secure to mention that you are from there?"

Four. Utilize your non-verbal communication (frame language) to show an hobby

While taking detail in a communicate with any individual, ensure you factor your frame towards them, maintain in contact, and slim in the direction of them. This tells your hobby in what the individual holds. If continuously shift focus or mind-set yourself far from them, they may be given this because the need to transport accomplish some issue unique.

5. Structure your inquiries in an open-ended format

At the factor whilst you make easy some pressing problems, make certain you country them efficaciously to incite a specific reaction from the opportunity person. Shut-ended questions like "Do you go to those activities frequently?" or "Are you hired inside the monetary vicinity?" spark off a short "nice" or "no" except if the individual needs to expound similarly. Thusly, pose inquiries like the ones at the identical time as you want to maintain up with the speak:

"How's the speech-composing technique?"

"How might also additionally need to you start off within the allotting corporation?"

"What might also need to you are pronouncing to really every person who hunts for a vocation in finance?"

"What's it like travelling on your paintings continuously?"

6. Exploit your present weather to foster talk elements

This is a respectable approach at the off risk that you do not understand the manner to interface with all people and keep a normal development of debate because it gets rid of the attention from you and them.

For instance:

"This is a particular one-of-a-kind occasion area. Have you been proper here formerly?"

"I see you went to the smorgasbord. What may also moreover you endorse?"

7. Offer records about yourself to provide unimportant inquiries concerning the opportunity character

Assuming that you are feeling as if you're doing the greater part of the speakme, you may make use of an inquiry to result in the other person to percent information about themselves or their concerns.

These are a few models:

"I'm from North Dakota. Where are you from?"

"I artwork in promoting correspondences. What's your profession?"

"I am Jordan. What's yours?"

8. Raise suitable modern trends

Assuming you're talking with any person from your area, you may make use of turning into contemporary traits to hold collectively collectively along with your talk. This may be an coming near

Seasonal occasion in your location, a few one of a kind eatery, or each different problem. Make an attempt no longer to examine political events to hold up together together together with your top notch functionality. Here are a few instances of the way to make use of modern tendencies to move your communicate along:

"Have you been to the October birthday party at the seventh avenue but?"

"Taylorstown really opened an Italian café and i've been reluctant to move. Have you long long past there however?"

Nine. Express out loud some thing you're wondering

While speaking with any person you do not know properly, you may experience such as you want to maintain a experience of convention round them. In any case, some of the time getting out a few aspect you think (sensibly talking) can assist the dialogue with proceeding. Here are a few instances of becoming proclamations to make:

"This cake is tasty."

"I can hardly ever wait until the climate situations get hotter."

"I'm so amped up for our drawing close send-off."

10. Acquaint them with a person else

To make a huge difference for the discussion but you may recognize you're walking out of remarks, deliver a person else into the communicate. A 1/three man or woman allow you to with developing new subjects of discussion to talk approximately.

Chapter 6: Eleven Methods For Remodeling Outsiders Into Companions

As of in recent times within the beyond, I noticed the area as a gap wherein no longer very many entryways opened for me. At first, I idea it modified into because of being very withdrawn. However, as time went on, I began out to battle with making companions.

I did no longer have a exquisite amount of them-and treasured open doors truly thumped more than one times each 12 months. That is the component at which I understood my worries originated from my loss of involvement and apprehension about in reality going out and conversing with human beings.

My couple of dearest companions commonly advised me to enroll in a membership or attend occasions. Individuals generally permit me realise in which to fulfill individuals. However, they in no way really knowledgeable me the brilliant manner to in reality make a dialogue.

In addition, I never in reality favored going to big activities. I'm unbiased and will extra frequently than no longer be overpowered whilst many people are close to. I like talking one-on-one.

So I decided directly to do matters as I might possibly determine upon. I started out out out speaking with outsiders on my faculty grounds and inside the metropolis because of the fact that I grow to be burnt out on last uninvolved.

It become horrifying for a commonly hesitant character like me, however I decided directly to battle the dread.

Extraordinary things arrive at the folks that will gamble with dismissal and located themselves obtainable.

By months of doing this, I made a few splendid companions, mainly thru beginning discussions.

It's an appealing mentality to have the selection to make a discussion with anybody.

There is normally the choice to talk with whom I need to speak with.

I asked human beings what drink they offered from the coffeehouse. I had been given some facts about her red bicycle. I asked that humans share suppositions on matters that impacted me.

Certain people have emerge as based upon me. Certain human beings remained close down. A variety of them constantly communicate themselves after I located the focal point on them. Others basically spoke back to my inquiry and left the communicate there.

These corporations legal me to look the manner to draw with individuals. For instance, I discovered that tone and non-verbal communique are a higher priority than saying the proper element.

Through my encounters, I determined that people are usually agreeable and satisfied to speak with you.

I've had the choice to satisfy a more quantity of human beings than I at any component anticipated virtually with the useful resource of starting up hooked up upon them.

That is the issue at which I placed that it relied on me to be proactive and make my entryways in place of whining that none had been beginning for me. It in fact trusted me to create my very own opportunities with the beneficial resource of interfacing with people.

Other than feeling extra associated, I revel in more cushty identifying that I can speak with whomever I need to. More open doors confirmed up by means of the use of networking with others. For instance, I had the choice to are trying to find images with some different accomplice basically due to the reality I related and inquired.

These are the eleven suggestions I found out approximately remodeling outsiders into companions:

1. Say the enchanted word: "Hello."

It sounds so common, but, it is the main large obstruction. You want to located your self available to begin a talk.

I noticed that people are inviting once you loosen subjects up. It's now not some thing that everyone wants to do because it takes highbrow fortitude to transport up to anybody you have got were given in no way met and start a talk. Nonetheless, a larger substantial form of humans are inviting than we normally expect. At the element even as you enjoy a person who is not, keep in thoughts that a few other character can be.

2. Detach yourself from the stop result.

When you do no longer count on to get any end end result, you could not be angry or outraged if everybody does not answer you.

There is a difference amongst apparent consequences and what certainly happens. How regularly have you ever pressured over a maximum pessimistic situation or situation truly to determine out that it turned out a long way advanced to what you predicted?

If I assume no end stop result from some thing I'm doing, then, I can be in the right second and change as it want to be.

3. Tolerate dismissal.

Assuming that they reject you, it's now not crucial to talk approximately you. It's approximately wherein they are at mentally, so do no longer remember it in reality. Within the occasion that they ignored the chance to accomplice with you, they exceeded up a few issue high-quality.

Give no damn to what the stranger thinks.

This is your life, and you reserve the choice to talk with whomever you need to speak with. Not anybody is honestly open. Permit them to be the way they'll be and suppose the way that they do, with out allowing it to project your fortitude.

Five. If you experience the dread, do it except.

Probably the most excellent manner to combat the worry is to do it more than as quickly as. Push via the dread and it will begin to revel in greater ordinary.

The dread may additionally in no manner simply die down, however on the off hazard which you hold on stopping through it, the pressure you are making can be greater great than the leftover dread. For example, after I feel alarmed via transferring towards absolutely everyone, I hold in mind a quiet 2d or a 2d that made me laugh. Then, at that element, the dread did now not sense so overwhelming any more.

6. Practice.

Relax assuming you appear like exceedingly off-kilter or forceful from the outset. Assuming your desires are legitimate, you can skip over that manner more and more whenever you attempt.

It's very much like a few component exclusive records in which it receives more sincere with education. A couple of my first discussions with outsiders felt unnerving and off-kilter, however, they added approximately no harm. It precipitated me to recognize what I predicted to address.

7. Make it about them.

Talk about their inclinations, suppositions, and thoughts. Then solution what they percentage.

The maximum pleasant way to maintain all and sundry intrigued with the useful resource of a discussion is to show an hobby in their life. Everybody likes to speak approximately themselves. Regardless of whether or now not you recognize a awesome deal about a specific difficulty, preserve to pose questions to get them.

Eight. Make them snigger.

Chuckling makes the speak a laugh and upbeat. Human beings recognize Discussing with one-of-a-type folks that purpose them to chortle.. So escape your head and make too much of not something mess around with it!

9. Attempt to find out their middle ardour.

Assuming you observe their eyes mild up after they communicate approximately something, pose more inquiries about that.

Assuming you find out a keyword that assists you with sorting out their interests, attempt to talk approximately that. For example, assuming I inquired "How's the climate?" They say, "extraordinary that it is hazy for the reason that. It's smarter to run in it." Then you could revel in loose to talk approximately taking walks.

10. Go out and grin!

Grinning offers a notable initial feeling. Practice in the replicate. Then, at that issue, grin at the arena.

I noticed that human beings loosened up as soon as I smiled first. At the issue once I stored grinning during the communicate, they grinned lower lower back and absolutely freed themselves up to a extra profound dialogue.

11. Imagine that the opposite individual is as of now your associate.

This way you may address them that manner in preference to appearing to be bizarre and being agreeable round any character is the exceptional way to start some other fellowship.

Take a hazard in recent times and talk with each one of a kind person. At the point even as you are agreeable to any man or woman, they will most regularly be amicable yet again.

Chapter 7: Step Commands To Forestall An Easygoing Speak

These dialogue enders are exquisite to apply frequently:

With friends and companions

Within the direction of parties and extraordinary get-togethers

Eventually of arbitrary discussions with outsiders

Beginning with...

#1: Raise tentative arrangements

"Do have a extraordinary time at the side of your XYZ plans!"

Inquire as to whether they've got any plans both this give up of the week or after the occasion. This places them in a destiny mode so they'll be organized to speak about destiny topics (like consummation the speak). It's moreover an wonderful chance to get to understand their entertainment sports for positive they like to do in their greater strength.

Sway degree: Medium

#2: Make an association together

"I'd very masses need to continue with our go to over lunch together!"

Would you like to get coffee from the books or get lunch collectively? This is a exceptional approach to showing co with a shared hobby in each other.

Sway Level: High

#3: Look into the space

Individuals listening invest the large majority in their strength checking the speaker out. A remarkable technique for telling the speaker you are no longer so intrigued is turning away your look, glancing round on the weather. More regularly than now not, they may get on this signal.

Sway Level: Low

#4: Utilize every distinct issue

"Something I wanted factor out before I pass is... "

This is one greater first-rate technique for trying no longer to be impolite, however further, growing the dialogue a chunk longer.

Sway Level: Medium

#five: Check in with the host

"I these days began to recognize I actually have no longer made proper acquaintance with the host however! I want to skip at this point. Great conversation with you!"

Notice that you actually need to find the host of the event. If it is a wonderful setting, this may clearly assist your societal feature and noticed ubiquity.

Sway Level: Medium

#6: Arch your foot within the direction of the entryway

A incredible many human beings realize that once your toes are pointing within the course of the left, you want to be anyplace but right right here. Fortunately, a first-rate many humans get in this set off.

Sway Level: Medium

#7: Distance your self

Back up, frequently. Slowly and intentionally. Not in the least does this make it more tough to impart, however they'll possibly get the belief.

Sway Level: Medium

#8: Review a story

"I'm so satisfied we met. A debt of gratitude is so as for sharing that story; it become so attractive. It's been notable!"

Did they specify an interesting / extraordinary / off-kilter/first-rate tale this is noteworthy? Bringing it up continues the feelings excessive and is a simple method for liking the alternative person.

Sway Level: High

#9: Reword the very last component they said

"oh, so you have a honestly pleasant art work place of work. That is really exquisite! Want to talk extra, but, I actually need to run soon."

This technique is specially precious for the folks who appear to speak unendingly.

Sway Level: Low

#10: Really check your watch

"I surely saw the time! It's getting past due. It modified into a pleasure meeting you!"

A more sincere method, this one is an inexpensive giveaway. The unique individual can also moreover directly get on this signal, or you may be extra clean via the usage of expressing the time.

Sway Level: Low

#11: Incorporate a period predicament

"I need to move proper far from now, however I'd very an lousy lot want to be aware about any other story."

This is a extra unobtrusive model of the simplest above. Fix in a reduce-off date to the talk so each of you've got more than one more minutes to wrap subjects up

Sway Level: Medium

#12: Excuse your self

"Please, excuse me... "

You do no longer really want to specify why you want to pardon your self. It's first-rate. Maybe you really need to talk with a few different man or woman. Or alternatively you have got have been given somewhere to go. Or then again possibly you've got got were given an lousy example of the runs. Regardless, you have made your purpose understood, and the "why" aspect may be left unsure.

Sway Level: Low

#13: Converse with a associate or partner

"Oh, there is my associate round there! It's been a pleasure speaking with you, however I must find out him."

In the event which you see any person you're acquainted with, pursue them! This can help your recognition due to the fact you show you've got got were given companions. On the opportunity hand, this will imply that some different person is extra massive or invigorating than them, this is the motive you are leaving anyways.

Sway Level: Medium

#14: The associate have a study

I ought to move, but permit you to recognize mother / partner / accomplice i said greetings!

Is your associate now not right right here to make all of the difference? No problems if each of you've got a common colleague or companion, sincerely inform your communicate accomplice you stated howdy to them the following time they see them.

Sway Level: Medium

#15: Pass on them to what they were doing

"Nice speakme with you! I'll bypass on you to do your shopping for now."

This is a totally treasured method assuming you hindered someone doing a motion prior to taking part inside the communicate.

Sway Level: Low

#16: Give them a handshake

Did you comprehend a handshake may be implemented to give up a speak, no longer simply starting one? Broaden your hand out and cling tight for them to famend it. This is also an top notch method for infusing instead extra oxytocin into the speak previous to leaving.

Sway Level: High

#17: Observe a weather sign

"Amazing, I certainly observed the clock and cited how past due it is! We have to look up a few other time."

Check the climate and get motivation. It thoroughly can be some thing-even the food at the table reminding you to put together supper.

Sway Level: Low

#18: Take a seat

"Hello, it is been a protracted day of popularity! I will skip sit down down down in the imply time. It's been notable meeting you!"

An pleasant approach for getting away assuming it's miles been an extended day. On the downside, this furthermore submits you to truly plunking down for some time, conceivably making you skip up a few interest or retaining you caught to the seating segment.

Sway Level: Low

#19: Return home

"Goodness is time slipping away out. I need to transport lower lower back domestic earlier than my sweetheart will become stressed!"

It's overdue out, you want to put together dinner in your soul mate, you have were given payments to pay-as long as your purpose is straightforward (better in the occasion that it's miles legitimate), permit all of it out! However, make a component to in reality cross returned home. Back in my university days, I executed this cause at a networking event... honestly to fulfill precisely the same character an hour after the reality on the café close by. Off-kilter!

Sway Level: Low

#20: Pleasantly come to a selection a mobile phone choice

"I'd very tons need to preserve speaking, however, I need to determine a smartphone desire at the existing time. Would we've got the capability to talk later?"

Is it past due? Would you have the potential to call your mother or a partner? This works assuming you clearly have someone you can talk with. If no longer, there are trade tactics (see next tip)...

Sway Level: Low-Medium

#21: The email look at-up

"I had some true times speaking with you! I will ensure to offer you an email."

No, this talk might now not really paintings all through the Nineties. You can anyhow electronic mail human beings nowadays!

Sway Level: High

#22: Give Thanks

"A debt of gratitude for chatting! Farewell now, I need to go."

This is the maximum right away-to-the-factor approach to respectfully leave a dialogue. The key's to visually be part of and say it in an earnest manner. You may be fairly first rate for your dreams and furthermore seem like distinctly earnest.

Chapter 8: How To Master The Art Of Small Talk

How do you sense about small talk? Have you ever prolonged past to a networking event and spent the higher part of the midnight loitering within the back of the buffet

Table due to the truth you have been uncertain of the way to begin up a communique? Perhaps the perception of having to face each different dinner collecting looking for something clean to mention makes you get away in a chilly sweat? Maybe you fall into the organisation that regards small chat as a vital evil that desires to be suffered earlier than you could growth the problem onto a deeper diploma? Talking about the weather or the ultra-modern Netflix display also can appear like a waste of time but these easy exchanges may be the building blocks for deeper friendships. Learning to certainly be given, or even love, small chat might also moreover do wonders for your private and expert life. Whether you are at a networking occasion, dinner party, or on a primary date, reading the artwork of small communicate can open up new probabilities and assist you create actual connections.

In her e-book, The Fine Art of Small Talk, Debra Fine says that after we avoid small speak and informal talks with our pals, co-employees, or maybe the check-out clerk at the grocery maintain, we lessen the form of profound conversations we get to have inside the future. Even worse, no longer taking component in informal communication would possibly make us appearance unpleasant, bloodless, or indifferent. If you war with small speak due to the fact you're socially hectic or discover it difficult to count on of things to say. Here are some strategies to help you decorate in self notion:

1. Pretend you're speakme to an vintage pal.

I go together with the 'in no manner met a stranger' approach. I chat to absolutely every person like i've recognized them for years. Praised because the finest advice from the thread, the perception of treating small conversation as if you were speakme with someone you're close to friends with is as easy as a shift in point of view.

2. Assume the exceptional in humans.

When you meet a person, ASSUME they'll be lovely. ASSUME that they will be your friend. You also can introduce your self LATER. For example, this night I turn out to be at a grand birthday celebration. Sat close to a person I didn't understand. I didn't introduce myself and ask them to be my pal. I noted the meal become terrific and made a funny tale about how some little children have been Googling their cuisine. You've genuinely been taught about stranger hazard because you were a youngster, but the ones instincts acquired't do you any genuine while you're seeking to get to understand people. The faster you open your self, the greater likely it is that you could bypass the silly "what's your call and what do you do?" Speak.

3. Know that nobody is right with names.

Here's the factor no person realizes. Everybody is horrible at names. Everybody. So announcing 'I'm so sorry, what's your name all another time?' isn't so horrible. A lot of the time it gives them the opportunity to ask you the same in view that, once more, everybody is horrible at names. This one is a bit of a relief to concentrate approximately. Turns out memorizing names is hard for every body. So, don't revel in lousy if you need a short reminder. You likely wouldn't hold it in opposition to each person, and it's dubious every body need to preserve it toward you.

Four. Keep the focus in your conversation accomplice.

Make humans communicate about themselves. One of the toughest subjects approximately small chat is locating something to speak about besides the climate. But, skilled networkers have found that maximum humans enjoy talking approximately themselves. Take it and run with it.

Five. Make connections and supply compliments.

And percent things that pertain to what they're pronouncing, in particular if it demonstrates a few similarity. After something narrative they inform, you normally need to answer one of strategies: (1) 'That's exceptional and is so much like what I professional!' (i.E. I'm including you!) [or] (2) 'That's top notch and i've never met a person who completed it!' (i.E. You are a unique snowflake and I'm inspired!) A dialogue is a -manner street, so don't neglect to create a few connections with the testimonies you're paying attention to. If all else fails, praises are commonly universally warmly common.

6. Read up on modern-day sports.

Stay up to speed with news and modern-day occasions and those will remember your IQ has extended. You with a chunk of achievement do this already. (If now not, proper here are a few tips for a way to encompass it into your ordinary.) To make yourself a small chat prepared, in reality step it up a degree and function an knowledgeable attitude. With that being stated, don't provide you with an incendiary idea without a doubt to have one. Instead, keep present day-day-day on what you care approximately, and your enthusiasm and expertise will come via.

7. Be concerned.

Not an professional, but I understand the name of the game: powerful small talkers are folks who are actually interested in the tiny facts of different humans's lives. I can faux for a time, however I normally soon revel in bored and irritated unless I'm talking to a in fact exciting individual. Great small talkers are the folks that can discover the interesting factors of all people and admire them. There's now not some thing that makes someone extra attractive than being involved. Period. So, in region of feigning exhilaration about a person's coming near near relocation, try to discover a subject you every care about—

whether or now not it's future weekend plans, a appropriate canine, a contemporary TV software program, or the food being exceeded round.

Eight. Put your self handy as a good buy as feasible.

Practice. The extra you do it, the better you come to be at it. This isn't the recommendation you've got been hoping for, however that's the truth. You'll broaden better at small chatting the extra you do it and that's all.

9. Keep calm and keep on.

Just loosen up. Most humans aren't evil/terrible/out to get you. Just deliver up not unusual topics, sports sports, movies, and track, tremendous to discover something you can chat about. All being stated, in the long run, a small chat isn't a huge hassle, so allow's in fact no longer make it a large deal. Relax and realise that handiest you are stressing out over or possibly aware of all of the minor errors you remember you're making in a speak. With know-how that spans the patron goods, financial, and amusement sectors, Vern is continuously on the bypass and striving to combine his pursuits alongside together with his large career. An unashamed data addict, he is continuously doing his excellent to live on top of factors with the entirety taking region round the arena. One of his many lifestyles interests is to have an award or scholarship named after him.

10. Adopt a increase mentality.

Don't fear if the small verbal exchange doesn't come effects to you. With the perfect angle, without a doubt everybody can discover ways to be an extraordinary communicator. In specific, a improvement mentality will will permit you to assignment from your consolation location and stay endorsed whilst you meet obstacles. People with a improvement attitude feel that they could beautify with practice even as human beings with a fixed mentality recollect that someone's traits and competencies are defined at begin.

11. Use frame language to increase rapport.

Use your body language at a few degree within the communicate to suggest that you are interested and worried. Visual clues are specially huge even as you are paying attention to the opposite man or woman. Make eye touch, smile (except the problem being addressed is of a important or gloomy tone), and maintain targeted at the speaker. Try no longer to transport your arms or area your palms for your hips and avoid fidgeting or observing during the room to look what awesome people are doing. Show that you are listening with the useful useful resource of nodding, making a song, and asking elaborating questions.

12. Prepare some ice-breakers.

Preparation is a crucial trouble of creating small chats each much less difficult and extra fun. It is ordinary to be hesitant in advance than starting a verbal exchange and plenty of human beings revel in greater cushty in the occasion that they have got some move-to icebreakers underneath their sleeve. Here are a few tips:

Use the scenario, placing, or event as your beginning thing. For instance: "What brings you proper proper here nowadays?" Or "What did you believe you studied of the live overall performance/play/lecture?"

Pay the opportunity man or woman a compliment. For example: "I adore your footwear. It is brilliant to look a person carrying coloration."

Find some commonplace floor. For instance: "I work in advertising too. How prolonged have you ever been in the industry?"

Thirteen. Be an engaged listener.

You can trust that you are a first rate listener however in a talk are you truely focused on what the alternative character is pronouncing or are you genuinely searching out an opening to speak? If someone is detailing their contemporary getaway, it is probably tempting to leap in with a holiday-associated narrative of your non-public as quickly as they pause to take a breath. Being an engaged listener implies paying attention to recognise in desire to answer. The subsequent time you talk to a person, avoid the selection to place the highlight on your self. Instead, cognizance on what is being said and offer appropriate questions that allow the possibility man or woman to intricate on the problem.

14. Ask open-ended inquiries.

Try to invite open-ended questions in desire to shut to-ended inquiries that simply want a 'positive' or 'no' reaction. For example in choice to asking 'do you experience your interest?' you could inquire ' How did you get into your line of labor?' or 'what do you respect excellent about your interest? ' People regularly pick talking approximately themselves but be careful for asking inquiries which is probably too intimate at the same time as you're although at the getting to know every specific degree.

15. Steer away from tough troubles.

The purpose of small chat is to hold matters mild. Avoid delicate and probable contentious subject matters which incorporates politics, religion, or coins. As nicely as discussing your environment, more powerful small communicate subjects include entertainment (TV applications, movies, books, plays, and so on.), paintings and lifestyle, sports sports activities, and adventure. Here inside the UK, the climate is a in particular commonplace small talk concern rely and despite the fact that it can now not seem like the most interesting communique opener, it's far sincerely a safe difficulty whilst chatting to new human beings.

16. Finish in a tone of thankfulness.

If you're new to small chat, terminating a communique may also revel in as difficult as starting one. Debra Fine says that after it is time to head, you could thank the possibility individual for their time, and data or simply observation how an lousy lot you desired speakme to them. Expressing thankfulness will now not only depart the opportunity man or woman feeling appropriate approximately themselves but additionally complements the opportunity of creating an prolonged-time period bond. If you would love to look the character over again, you ought to say so and follow up with an e-mail, textual content, or smartphone call in the subsequent day or .

How to Start a Conversation with Anyone and What to Say

Did that public speaking is regularly rated because of the truth the primary difficulty people are afraid of? But at the identical time as getting up on a level in front of an target market may be nerve-wracking, many humans locate putting in a communique one-on-one clearly as intimidating. Maybe it's far the CEO of your enterprise employer, a new colleague, the man inside the mail room, the girl from IT, or a stranger in the street. Whomever you need to speak to, there is a way to strike up a communication. And the terrific news is that it receives less complicated with workout. Try those conversation starters to speak to in reality all people:

1. Skip the small communicate.

"What's up with this weather?" and "How 'bout them [insert local sports team]?" are as awful as tacky choose out-up strains as regards to beginning a communication. Avoid worn-out subjects. Every scenario is unique, so you need to be able to locate a very unique conversation starter.

2. Ask for his or her opinion.

Everyone has one! For a person you do not understand nicely, start with slight subjects similar to the food, the track, the environment, and so on. "Do you need your margaritas with salt or without? Do you watch horror movies? Do you want this song?" It's in all likelihood awesome to stay faraway from certainly sticky topics like politics except you recognize the person very well.

3. Ask for his or her recommendation or pointers.

This works thoroughly even as commenting on someone's outfit or add-ons, as in "What a fantastic tie! Where did you get it?" or at the food, as in, "Everything appears pinnacle. What are you having?"

4. Ask them a query — this is simple to answer.

This is brilliant at the same time as you comprehend or discover that a person has knowledge in a particular location. If you're speakme for your organisation's IT guy, for instance, you can ask him whether or not or now not he's the man who installs hardware or software. But keep away from asking all people to offer an reason for some component fantastic complex or concerned; if that is wherein the communique leads, incredible, but asking a complex query up the the front can feel stressful.

Five. Comment at the surroundings.

No rely in which you are, there are matters to touch upon: the track, the meals, the lighting, the visitors, and so on. Even in case you are caught in an elevator with someone, you can touch upon the music, the rate, the crowdedness, and so forth.

6. Ask for an replace.

If you understand someone a bit or recognize them by means of way of recognition, ask for an update on a few factor they've got been doing, as an instance, "Oh, Mary noted you've got been taking swing dance instructions. How's that going?"

7. Ask open-ended questions every time viable.

If your question can be replied with a easy sure or no, don't be surprised if that is what you get. Having take a look at-up questions prepared also can help the communique glide. If you are asking what kind of meals they will be having, as an instance, you could examine up with, "That sounds exquisite. Do what kind of wine may pass nicely with that?" Almost everything may be followed up with, "Why?" (Just do no longer ask it too generally and end up sounding like a three-12 months-antique!)

Eight. Ask a hypothetical question.

These can be fantastic conversation starters, however try to tie them into some trouble occurring on the occasion or in cutting-edge sports to avoid seeming too random. You may want to in all likelihood say a few issue like, "I simply saw this movie wherein all the laws were revoked for in the future. What may also want to you do if there were no criminal guidelines for an afternoon?"

Nine. Ask approximately their kids, pets, or hobbies.

People love to speak about the things that are essential to them. If that your boss likes to sail, asking him approximately his state-of-the-art enjoy is a surefire manner to get him speaking.

Chapter 9: How To Begin A Conversation With The Aid Of The Use Of Listening

Listening is one of the maximum essential talents you may have. How properly you pay attention has a number one impact on your job effectiveness and the great of your relationships with others. For example:

We listen to attain facts.

We concentrate to apprehend.

We listen for leisure.

We pay interest to analyze.

Given all of the listening that we do, you will assume we'd be proper at it! Most people are not, and research shows that we simplest recollect amongst 25 percentage and 50 percent of what we pay interest, as defined with the aid of manner of Edgar Dale's Cone of Experience. That way that at the identical time as you speak to your boss, colleagues, clients, or accomplice for 10 mins, they be aware of much less than half of of the communication. Turn it round and it well-knownshows that at the same time as you're receiving directions or being furnished with records, you are not listening to the complete message each. You preference the important factors are captured in your 25-50 percentage, however what if they're not?

Listening is a functionality that we are able to all advantage from enhancing. By becoming a higher listener, you can improve your productiveness, in addition to your functionality to persuade, persuade and negotiate. What's extra, you may keep away from conflict and misunderstandings. All of these are critical for place of job success!

Tip:

Good conversation competencies require a immoderate diploma of self-attention. Understanding your fashion of speakme will pass an extended way in the direction of helping you to create appropriate and lasting impressions with others.

About Active Listening

The way to decorate your listening skills is to exercise "lively listening." This is in that you're developing a aware try to listen no longer exceptional the terms that some other man or woman is announcing however, greater importantly, the complete message being communicated. To do this, you want to be aware of the possibility individual very carefully. You cannot allow your self to come to be distracted with the aid of something else can be taking place round you, or with the aid of the use of way of forming counterarguments while the alternative individual stays talking. Nor are you able to permit yourself to become bored, and lose attention on what the alternative man or woman is pronouncing.

Tip:

If you're finding it particularly difficult to pay attention on what someone is pronouncing, try repeating their words mentally as they're announcing them. This will beautify their message and can help you live focused. To beautify your listening abilties, you want to permit the alternative man or woman understand which you are being attentive to what they are announcing. To apprehend the significance of this, ask your self if you've ever been engaged in a communique even as you puzzled if the opportunity man or woman became paying attention to what you have been pronouncing. You surprise in case your message is getting at some stage in, or if it's miles even profitable persevering with to talk. It looks as if talking to a brick wall and it is a few element you need to avoid.

Acknowledgment can be some thing as easy as a nod of the pinnacle or a clean "uh-huh." You aren't always agreeing with the character, you're surely indicating which you are listening. Using frame language and one-of-a-type symptoms and signs and symptoms and signs and symptoms to renowned you are listening also can help you to pay interest. Try to reply to the speaker in a way at the manner to encourage them to keep talking, so you can get the facts which you need. While nodding and "uh-huh" says you are involved, an occasional question or remark to recap what has been stated furthermore communicates which you are listening and facts his message.

Tip:

Be aware that lively listening can deliver others the have an impact on that you receive as actual with them even if you don't. It's additionally critical to avoid using lively listening as a checklist of moves to observe, in region of listening. It may additionally moreover help to exercising Mindful Listening if you find out that you lose recognition frequently.

Becoming an Active Listener (Hear What People Are Saying)

There are five key energetic listening strategies you may use to help you end up a more powerful listener:

1. Pay Attention.

Give the speaker your undivided interest, and famend the message. Recognize that non-verbal communication furthermore "speaks" loudly.

Look on the speaker directly.

Put apart distracting thoughts.

Don't mentally prepare a rebuttal!

Avoid being distracted through way of environmental factors. For instance, trouble conversations.

"Listen" to the speaker's frame language.

2. Show That You're Listening.

Use your frame language and gestures to reveal which you are engaged.

Nod sometimes.

Smile and use other facial expressions.

Make sure that your posture is open and exciting.

Encourage the speaker to keep with small verbal comments like sure, and "uh-huh."

Three. Provide Feedback.

Our filters, assumptions, judgments, and beliefs can distort what we pay hobby. As a listener, your characteristic is to apprehend what's being stated. This can also require you to mirror on what is being said and to invite questions.

Reflect on what has been stated via paraphrasing. "What I'm hearing is...," and "Sounds like you are saying...," are awesome techniques to mirror.

Ask inquiries to make clear certain elements. "What do you imply while you are saying... ." "Is this what you suggest?"

Summarize the speaker's remarks periodically.

Tip:

If you find your self responding emotionally to what a person said, say so. And ask for greater records: "I won't be facts you successfully, and I find myself taking what you stated individually. What I concept you without a doubt said is XXX. Is that what you intended?"

4. Suspend judgment and enlarge grace.

Interrupting is a waste of time. It frustrates the speaker and barriers the complete knowledge of the message.

Allow the speaker to complete each aspect in advance than asking questions.

Don't interrupt with counter arguments.

Five. Respond Appropriately.

Active listening is designed to encourage appreciate and know-how. You are gaining statistics and mindset. You add no longer some thing with the aid of using attacking the speaker or otherwise setting her down.

Be candid, open, and honest to your reaction.

Assert your reviews respectfully.

Treat the alternative man or woman in a manner that you anticipate they'll want to be dealt with.

How to Enhance your Listening Skills

It takes a whole lot of focus and determination to be an engaged listener. Old conduct are tough to trade, and in case your listening capabilities are as awful as many humans are, then you may want to do a whole lot of strive to break those horrific patterns. These are a few essential techniques you may employ to increase your lively listening competencies:

1. Allow humans the courtesy of quiet even as they are speakme.

When we are lessen off even as the usage of we get avenue rage; even as we're lessen off while chatting, we get conversation fury. One of the handiest strategies to supply unsightly emotions in a speak is to interrupt a person. Whenever you enjoy the impulse to percentage your element of view, alternative that with an "mhm" or "yeah, right" to demonstrate you are listening.

2. Maintain a comfortable and courteous tone on the identical time as you are speakme.

If you are passionate about some thing it's miles most effective natural to emerge as active and active. What seems like right emotion to you, but, may come to be threatening to your conversational companion, specifically in case you function with a loud voice and hand movements that border on pointing.

3. Come with an open mind, eager to analyze and beautify.

Part of the pleasure of meeting new humans and having discussions is to boom our horizons. We discover new places to benefit new research, and we look at new literature to ignite gaining knowledge of. Think of talks like a bit of every, and include the attitude described with the useful resource of Bill Nye,

"Everyone you'll ever meet is aware of a few factor you don't."

Four. Listen to others as you need them to be aware of you.

Our first three standards can truely be described with the resource of this version of the Golden Rule. Think about the manner you want to be handled in speak - with decency and appreciate - and pledge to cope with your associate in that manner. Listen to and do not forget others' perspectives in advance than providing your very own. It is natural to want to specific your ideas and contribute your cents. For many listening settings, despite the fact that, your point of view isn't always important. People don't continuously communicate to you to pay attention your facet of the tale. More normally, individuals want to percentage their element of the story and on the way to concentrate to it with out interruption.

Five. Be gift and interested in desire to considering a way to reply.

Steven Covey is generally said as affirming, "Most people do now not concentrate with the cause to recognize; they pay attention with the cause to react. They're every speakme or organized to speak." Being gift is taking note of the alternative person, in fact intrigued about them and their narrative. When you're gift and inquisitive, the speak is probably greater big for each you and your companion.

6. Fully take part, freed from distractions.

One of the number one distractions nowadays is our mobile cellular telephone, and a have a observe well-knownshows that virtually its presence may additionally alter our ability to be gift. Cell phones have an off button for a motive, and if this communicate is large enough to seize your attention then it is vital sufficient to make use of that button. Stay focused to your speak accomplice, keeping eye contact with them and not your surroundings.

7. Restate what you heard to deepen comprehension, using "I" terms ("What I heard you are pronouncing modified into" or "The manner I recognize your stance is").

Although you can imply you're focused by way of the use of ridding yourself of distractions and preserving eye contact, research has examined that what you are announcing as a listener is essential. When you use restatements to signify how you have got interpreted the speaker, you permit them to both concur ("Yes, that's what I intended!") Or to offer an cause of their stance ("Actually, what I supposed emerge as ..."). Importantly, restatements are not repeats, that means you need to no longer simply repeat precisely what they said. Instead, unique it to your own words, and show that this is your understanding through the use of starting up your sentence with "I."

Eight. Ask substantial and courteous inquiries, unfastened from prejudice, assumption, or bias.

A wonderful-fireplace technique to begin someone speaking is to invite them a question - the way that our language is prepared, questions call for replies. But be careful! Don't feature your queries as a form of judgment (e.G., "Don't you accept as true with you studied that your factor of view is old skool?"). We are judged enough within the route of our day; strive our great not to contribute to it.

Nine. Seek to discover comparable pursuits and regions of agreement with the beneficial useful resource of concentrating extra on why than what, greater on non-public studies than viewpoints.

There isn't any faster manner to complete a talk or amplify to battle of words than to begin reciting information. In brand new, information want to now not be your first line of safety, despite the truth that they will be your first move-to. Research shows people are drastically greater willing to explore severa factors of view on the same time as there may be an emotional connection, a dating. Rather than start with "how are we one-of-a-type" start with "what are our shared center values." Get your partner to narrate personal testimonies, and pay interest for areas of comparable enjoy, and possibilities to attach on a human diploma. Avoid discussing positions till you get to apprehend each one-of-a-type and may discover what makes your companion tick. This is as right in talks approximately routine troubles as it's miles in conversations about contentious ones.

Chapter 10: How To Keep A Conversation Going

Keeping a communication going may be a venture. Luckily, there are clean strategies you could use to maintain the alternative character engaged and involved. Prove your interest by the use of asking pinnacle questions and listening. Then, discover a rhythm that lets in you to construct rapport with the opportunity man or woman. Make nice to display open frame language that makes the opportunity man or woman sense comfortable in some unspecified time in the future of the verbal exchange.

Things You Should Know

Create hobby by means of manner of using choosing subjects the opposite man or woman enjoys, asking open-ended questions, encouraging them, and listening actively.

Try to persuade them to snort and forestall yourself from filtering your terms; don't be terrified of silence, and contact out awkwardness as it takes area.

Maintain comfortable, open, and confident frame language even as absolutely dealing with your communication companion to make eye touch.

Step 1: Choosing Interesting Topics.

1. Choose topics you understand the opposite character cares approximately.

In modern-day, people like to speak about themselves and their hobbies. You can keep your communique rolling with the aid of manner of sticking to subjects you recognize the possibility character likes.

Before assembly up with someone, recall 3 predetermined topics you could fall again on if communication lags. Remind yourself of any cutting-edge journeys, paintings occasions, or relationships your friend has instructed you about.

Ask questions on their college or paintings, passions or pursuits, family and friends, or their ancient past (in which they got here from or their family statistics).

You can also use context cues from earlier elements of the conversation to determine whether or not or no longer or now not to drop a topic or maintain it. For example, if earlier, the person lit up on the same time as talking approximately using bulls, you could ask them about unique bull riders, cowboy lifestyle, or what it became similar to the first time they rode.

If you aren't superb what the individual would really like to talk approximately, ask questions which you may enjoy being requested your self.

2. Ask open-ended questions.

"Yes," or "no" fashion questions can near down the conversation whilst others open the doors for added possibilities. Stick to open-ended questions that permit the opportunity individual to hard as heaps as they'd like.

On the opposite hand, open-ended questions call for extra from the answerer. For example, in place of asking the query "So, you studied a yr remote places in 2006, is that proper?," attempt asking "What turn out to be it like studying remote places?" The 2nd question will provide the man or woman you are speakme to extra room to complicated on their answer.

If you do ask a "sure" or "no" close to-ended question, recover through pronouncing some thing like "Tell me extra."

Fun revolutionary icebreaker questions embody "What have been you want in excessive university?" or "what is one element people is probably simply amazed to look at you?"

3. Listen attentively to what they will be pronouncing.

Listening is as essential as speaking in terms of retaining a communication. Actively listening lets in you to pay interest the alternative character's attitude. Wait till the man or woman has completed speaking in advance than saying whatever. Then, sum up what they stated to reveal you have got been listening via way of saying a few thing like "It seems like..."

If you misunderstand a few a part of the message, ask a clarifying query, like "Are you saying...?"

If you're an top notch listener, you may use any unexplored subjects touched on in advance in the conversation to maintain topics moving. For example, you may likely say, "Earlier I heard you issue out..."

Express empathy as you pay attention with the beneficial aid of placing your self inside the one in all a kind man or woman's footwear.

Four. Encourage them to hold speaking.

The awesome listeners don't virtually sit down down there and stare on the speaker throughout a conversation. They engage with them, with out interrupting, thru the usage of encouragers. These might be little noises of approval like "Ahh" or "Oh?" Encouragers may moreover encourage the man or woman to preserve speaking, which incorporates on the same time as you're saying "And?"

Encouragers additionally can be nodding or mirroring the alternative man or woman's facial expression, which incorporates searching surprised or disenchanted.

Step 2: Developing a Nice Rhythm

1. Don't clear out.

One of the motives maximum conversations fall brief is each human beings are filtering what they want to or shouldn't say. You begin to anticipate you've run out of topics and you could't tell if something that involves mind is appropriate or first-rate sufficient. During the ones times, follow the technique of simply blurting out whatever you're thinking with out censoring it.

For example, there's an extended silence and you consider you studied how uncomfortable your feet are on your heels. Blurting out "Geez, the ones heels are killing my feet!"

may appear bizarre. But that sincere statement need to reason a communication about a feminist factor of view of now not carrying immoderate heels or a talk approximately a time whilst a person fell due to the fact they had been sporting ridiculously immoderate heels.

2. Call out the awkwardness.

Even the amazing conversations run into roadblocks that threaten to throw things off route. The nice answer for that is naming it and moving ahead. Pretending the soreness isn't there also can push the opposite person away.

For example, in case you misspoke and stated a few issue offensive, at once once more-track and express regret. Don't act adore it didn't seem.

3. Make them giggle.

Humor is a extraordinary manner to hold the conversation going. It additionally permits you forge a bond with the alternative man or woman. We're more likely to laugh with our buddies, so making the alternative person snort office work a kinship with them. You don't need to bust out with a comedian story to make a person snicker. Well-timed sarcasm and wit can do the venture definitely as efficaciously. For instance, you hold bringing up your hobby in anime to the opportunity person. After the 1/3 point out, you could say, "So, I wager I want to prevent bringing up anime earlier than you observed I'm a freak... I am. I'm an anime freak. I convey a fancy dress round with me of my favorite individual. Just kidding!"

Four. Go deeper collectively along with your questions.

After you have gotten the formalities out of the way, take the verbal exchange to a deeper diploma. Think of a communication like a meal: you devour the appetizers earlier than you dig into the primary direction and then dessert. Once you and the possibility character have prolonged beyond multiple rounds with superficial topics, skip further.

For example, you requested, "What do you do for a residing?" After a while, you may dig deeper with the aid of way of asking, "Why did you select out that profession?" Generally, "why" questions help you dig deeper into records that has already been shared. As you're asking greater intimate questions, pay near interest to cues about the other man or woman's comfort stage. If they begin to seem uncomfortable, decrease lower back up and ask lots lots less intimate questions. Try to live on pinnacle of modern-day activities so you typically have something to make contributions to a verbal exchange. You can ask a person their opinion on a present day-day political trouble or development in the global, for instance.

5. Don't fear silence.

Silence is useful in verbal exchange and shouldn't be averted just like the plague. It allows you capture your breath and procedure your mind. It also can sign a much-need trade of subject matter if topics emerge as stupid or too excessive. A few seconds of silence are really ordinary. Don't experience the need to hurry in and fill it. However, if silence will become too protracted, pivot to a modern day venture remember quantity thru the use of pronouncing, "I'm interested in listening to more about what you've got been saying earlier about..."

Step three: Maintaining Good Body Language

1. Display snug body language.

Good frame language is number one to helping the opportunity character enjoy comfortable and open to speakme to you. Sitting ramrod directly to your chair can also make the opposite man or woman uneasy. To show your comfort degree, smile gently and lean decrease back a piece in your chair for an angular posture. Or, prop yourself casually closer to a wall or column if you're fame. Another manner to reveal you're comfortable is through loosening up your shoulders. Drop them down and backward if they're traumatic.

2. Face the person you are speaking to.

A extraordinary verbal exchange includes a connection between you and the alternative character. You obtained't benefit that connection if you're handling a long way from them. Plus, turning your frame or your feet away demonstrates that you're equipped to go away. Instead, orient your body towards the alternative individual. To show off interest inside the route of high-quality factors of the communication, lean ahead towards the character.

3. Make eye contact.

Regular eye touch is crucial to keeping a verbal exchange going. You want to right now make eye contact on the start of the communication. Then, preserve it by using using looking into the alternative man or woman's eyes for approximately four to 5 seconds. Looking away is right sufficient, too!

Take a few seconds to survey your surroundings in advance than re-setting up eye touch once more. Aim for about half of of of the time at the same time as you're speaking and 70 percent of the time while you are listening. Sticking to this ratio enables you undergo in thoughts how an awful lot eye contact to make with out staring someone down.

4. Uncross your legs and arms.

Crossed arms and legs send the message that you're disinterested in what the alternative individual has to say. It also can make you appear guarded or shielding. If you've got have been given a dependancy of crossing your arms and legs, make a further attempt to loosen up them at your sides at some stage in a verbal exchange. It's perfectly okay if this does not experience ordinary to you in the starting. Give it a try. Over time, you could come to sense more snug.

5. Power-pose to undertaking self belief.

If you're not feeling too confident, you could feature your frame in a way that makes you appearance and enjoy self-assured. When sitting, attempt clasping your arms inside the decrease again of your head in an inverted "V." If you're standing, a brilliant way to strength-pose is via putting your hands in your hips in the course of the communique.

How to Become an Interesting Person

I changed into scared of being silly. Networking gatherings made me fear whether or no longer or not my small communique sucked. Coffee conferences had been further nerve-wracking. And as quickly as I spoke at team meetings, a single sleepy co-employee can also make me overlook about about my argument. But then, I began out being attentive to how the maximum interesting human beings spherical me saved others' interest. I diagnosed that in reality as you may discover ways to be a higher leader or greater a achievement negotiator, you can learn how to be greater attractive. And that's exceptional information for your career. When you're interesting, each person you meet—from your agency for your capability corporation partner, for your buddies wants to be spherical you. Not simplest will you increase greater connections, but the ones relationships can be an awful lot much less tough to preserve and deepen. You do now not want to be a millionaire, or a CEO, or an astronaut to capture humans's hobby – you could absolutely be you. It's an trouble of information a way to exhibit the competencies that make you tremendous from the individual subsequent to you. Some of those capabilities are:

1. Develop new skills.

Ensure that high-quality humans find out you exciting thru making your self beneficial whenever. That's why Quora client Anthony N. Lee advocates analyzing as many beneficial capabilities as you could, from net layout to sewing. That way, you may continuously be the skip-to person, whether or now not or not a pal desires to collect a internet web site for her new company or a blanket for her little one niece.

2. Be inquisitive.

One way to guarantee which you're now not thrilling is thru the usage of lowering yourself up into severa mind and perspectives. Instead, you have to actively are looking for for out smooth thoughts and reviews in order to have an effect at the way you consider you studied and revel in. Sudhir Desai emphasizes being a "lifelong learner." He writes: "Keep an open thoughts, be interested. Allow for a complex universe with severa interpretations. Learn topics to beautify and widen your mind."

Three. Learn how to tell a first rate narrative.

Maybe you've got amassed a ton of information and stories - but in case you cannot provide an explanation for them to distinctive humans, you are screwed. That's why Marcus Geduld argues you want to discover ways to be a storyteller: "You do now not without a doubt pour some thing is for your mind into the communicate; you actively mold it to make it attractive. ... Start thinking about your lifestyles as a gift you can provide to others. Wrap it inside the nicest paper you may find." Geduld says it method you need to learn how to look at your goal market to determine how lengthy they will be able to pay interest and tease your listeners with hints to the cease of the narrative. Interestingly, a current observe shows that guys who can inform a compelling narrative are also perceived as greater appealing via ladies. The studies authors suggest it's possible due to the reality outstanding storytellers may additionally look higher placed to steer people or earn authority.

4. Have 3 extremely good tales equipped to percentage.

Knowing how to tell a tale spontaneously is a beneficial capability — however in case you're scared about that, organized yourself with a few private tales you can use to boost an in any other case dull communication. Comedians do no longer definitely speak about a few issue even as they're onstage. They have their performance rehearsed. You do not really trot right proper into a challenge interview and say some factor's in your mind. Always hold 3 first-rate testimonies to be had that dependably amuse, enlighten, or have interaction. Listen to and be interested in what exclusive people are announcing.

5. Listen and provide compassion.

This concept have become popularized with the resource of Dale Carnegie in his 1936 conventional "How to Win Friends and Influence People." Carnegie wrote: "You may also need to make extra buddies in months with the aid of using the use of having inquisitive about exceptional people than you may in years with the beneficial resource of looking to get unique people interested by you." Quentin Hardy, a Googler and former editor for The New York Times wrote: "Listen carefully to humans and attempt with some compassion to recognize their intentions and behaviors. Few folks are virtually remarkable at this. Everyone will become almost infinite in their enjoy of lifestyles if we take note of them with sufficient creativeness. Working that out develops us. Wondering whether or not you're incorrect assist, too."

6. Ask first rate questions.

At a celebration, you do not want to speak an entire lot approximately yourself for others to enjoy you're fascinating. Instead, engage them in intense discourse approximately their way of life. "Ask big (not probing) inquiries, if suitable, about them and their pursuits and goals," advises Stephanie Vardavas. "Listen to the responses. Follow up with further practical communique and applicable questions (yet again, not prying) (again, no longer prying). By the forestall of the middle of the night, they may maintain in thoughts you as one of the maximum captivating people they ever met." Don't be ashamed to ask clean inquiries, both. As Evan Ratliff, a writer who is written for magazines like The New Yorker, informed Fast Company: "There's regularly no purpose in claiming you apprehend some element while you do not. As a reporter, the cause is to benefit facts, not to have an effect on your subjects. You'd assume that might be terrific in commercial enterprise, however it's far no longer." By asking the ones easy inquiries, you could land up impressing your new friends, anyways.

7. Say what you think.

Kat Li believes folks that do no longer announcement on or disagree with something is probably stupid. "You enjoy such as you can not even communicate with them," she writes. "You ought to strive to speak what you consider approximately effective subjects, despite the reality that different people might not discover it impossible to resist."

8. Follow your hobbies.

Instead of analyzing about a ton of dull things most effective to be educated, are searching for areas that you genuinely find out interesting. That way, you may seem passionate and interesting whilst discussing them with other human beings. "I do now not take into account it is as a good buy a query of looking to be thrilling as loads as it's far sincerely pursuing what you want, being an ardent student and collector of material that intrigues and thrills you," writes Renee Nay. Reading masses offers you a extra fascinating and sensitive view of the sector.

9. Read hundreds.

If you've got got had been given the money and time to tour the globe, fantastic. But even in case you don't, you may but discover about numerous cultures and historic times with the useful resource of reading some thing you can are looking for out. Books, blogs, journals - expose oneself to as many glowing stories and thoughts as viable. Based on a check of the final decade of research on the highbrow affects of analyzing fiction, Keith Oatley counseled The Washington Post: "People who have a study greater fiction had been higher at empathy and know-how others." "Read masses - it opens up numerous new worlds to us," says Chaitra Murlidhar.

10. Display a sense of humor.

Awdesh Singh advocates cultivating a sense of humor in your dealings with people. "Learn to peer the lighter side of life," he affords, "and construct a addiction to be thrilled even on your shortcomings." Bonus if you're seeking to affect a date: Research well-known fun men are seen via manner of ladies as extra attractive, in element due to the fact they appearance more clever.

11. Spend time with one-of-a-kind thrilling people.

Singh says that the enterprise corporation you maintain shapes your man or woman. "If you are inside the corporation organisation of silly human beings, upset people, or severe humans, you will grow to be like them quite rapid," he explains. "The equal is real when you have the company of charming humans." Consider becoming a member of a Meetup or similar organization of folks who are determined to take a look at their pastimes and pursuits.

12. Dig deep into genuinely one in each of your passions.

You may be tempted to end up a dabbler in numerous disciplines, acquiring a hint little little bit of information about everything. Instead, try gaining knowledge of hundreds approximately one trouble and showcasing your capabilities in that region. April Fonti says she reveals people exciting after they "truly pursue one project with wonderful ardour and depth over a prolonged period. They might be tremendously achieved scientists or truly silent loners. It does now not rely." The approach of improvisation also can enhance your verbal exchange abilities.

13. Take an improv beauty.

Comedian Bill Connolly knowledgeable Fast Company that reading the artwork of improvisation may additionally additionally assist beautify your verbal exchange skills in everyday existence. One cause why is that it makes you a higher listener, specializing in what the opportunity person is announcing in preference to what you're going to say next. Ken Gregg says: "Even if you're shy and don't have any motive of ever performing publicly, improv comedy will loosen you up, help you 'assume faster,' re-learn how to be playful (some thing maximum adults have lost), and make you sense greater snug developing a idiot of your self in the front of other people (a lifestyles potential that is available in on hand often) (a life ability that is available in on hand regularly). It may also additionally moreover open you up and assist you turn out to be extra involved whilst engaging with terrific people."

14. Be unorthodox.

Evan Asano thinks being interesting boils all the manner all the way right down to being in a few way remarkable from actually anyone else. He writes: "A buddy of mine after university did some thing no person's ever completed in advance than (as a minimum seemed) (at least recognised). He circumambulated Martha's Vineyard thru its beach/shore. It simplest took more than one days and some tenting tools. Two a long time later he no matter the truth that tells the tale." Still, now not clearly every person has the resources or the motivation to spark off on a document-breaking camping enjoy right now. So recollect the unusual reminiscences you have got already had. Maybe you have lived foreign places; possibly you promote art work responsibilities as a side gig; possibly you grew up with 10 siblings. There's actually a few factor, so keep digging.

15. Embrace your strangeness.

"We all have quirks," writes Del Singh. "It is part of our being. Interesting people precise their quirkiness." Dressing, speakme, and behaving like definitely everyone else might be type bit stupid - we are now not in junior excessive college anymore. So permit your freak flag fly, and do it with self perception.

Sixteen. Open as an entire lot as human beings.

Danielle Lan tells a private anecdote, the lesson of this is that no one will realise how intriguing you are till you tell them: "My accomplice has been appeared as stupid. He's sincerely a pretty intriguing character, with all his eccentricities and pursuits. The trouble is he never stocks together with his colleagues or buddies. " When requested 'How turn out to be your weekend?' His solution is usually, 'Fine'. He in all likelihood took part in a massive raid in his preferred MMO [massively multiplayer online game] in advance than searching a present day movie and finishing an exciting ebook. But he might not percentage that with sincerely each person.S" To be what others keep in mind as fascinating you need to proportion. That additionally implies you have to have the stuff to proportion. It's an excellent character who does sincerely not whatever and has no opinion on any given trouble. My idea is to open up." Indeed, studies exhibits that people like a few other better after they every display screen some thing private, in place of whilst sincerely one individual does.

17. Run with a specific crowd.

Perhaps the real reason you don't enjoy charming is which you're spending time with folks that don't appreciate you. In this form of state of affairs, you have to find out a ultra-modern organization that recognizes how an entire lot you want to contribute.

How to Build a Meaningful Connection

While era has made it less complicated to remain in touch with the outside worldwide, and even get reacquainted with prolonged-misplaced buddies, it has furthermore converted how we outline relationships.

Someone with 1,000 Facebook friends may also moreover additionally be given as actual with they will be a rock megastar. But, how lots of those "pals" can be there to assist them after they begin a corporation or go through a non-public catastrophe? I've determined that the extra effective you're at relationships collectively together with your circle of relatives, friends, and customers; the extra a achievement you will be in lifestyles with they all. Because of the frenzy and bustle of the twenty first century, it's far even extra critical than ever to growth those big styles of interplay. Want to recognise the way to carry out that? Follow those 25 guidelines.

1. Be thrilled with your self.

You can also moreover have heard this one earlier than, and there may be a motive for it - it stays the finest place to start. As Michelle Maros so simply places it in, Peaceful Mind, Peaceful Life, "Your connections outside will fail if you do now not have unconditional love and compassion for yourself."

2. Learn to concentrate and understand.

Throughout your lifestyles, you have got were given in reality confronted this problem. Your dad and mom in no manner listened. Your companion by no means listens. Your supervisor certainly could not comprehend or concentrate. George P.H. Writes in, Pick The Brain, that we may moreover hook up with others simply with the resource of the usage of taking note of them, hearing them out without interruption, and trying our first rate to recognize in which they're coming from.

3. Take the hit.

You can't usually take subjects in my opinion. We all have terrible days even as we strain out, rant, or yell at humans round us. My companion Kristy Rampton continuously strikes a chord in my memory "There are few matters in existence much less unselfish than taking a punch now after which from parents which might be having a horrible day. Sometimes human beings honestly need to vent."

4. Follow-up.

If you enjoy like you've got struck it off with a person, professionally or in my view, do not appearance in advance to them to get in touch with you. If you sense that there may be a possibility for a brand new connection, then ensure which you look at up. Keith Ferrazzi, author of "Never Eat Alone," says which you need to comply with up internal 48 hours after the initial come across.

Five. Be incredible.

Here's a short query. Would you prefer to spend time with someone who is a downer or someone upbeat? Barbara Fredrickson, a psychologist on the University of North Carolina, backs up the apparent via way of saying, in Psychology Today, that wonderful feelings help us "make bigger and extend" connections.

6. Grab lunch.

We're all busy, but are you too busy to stop and devour? Probably now not. Relationship guru Nate Bagley from Loveumentary feels that you need to "make the time" to prepare a lunch with a pal, acquaintance, or family member. This interest will offer enormous rewards.

7. Don't be a person else.

I adore this headline from Adrian Savage in lifehack: "If you can't accept as real with your self, why need to others be given as authentic with you?"

Eight. Take stock of the connections you have.

Some partnerships are destined to final for a long time. Other relationships may additionally only hold because it's cushty and feels stable. Take an stock of the connections and feature a examine which ones you could want to comprehend onto and people you could allow pass. Getting rid of superfluous connections provides you the opportunity to invite new partnerships into your life.

9. Pick up the cellphone.

Texts, electronic mail, and Facebook remarks are best sometimes, but there is nothing like having a real chat with someone. Don't hesitate to select out up the phone and supply your buddy or peer a name to test in and notice how they will be doing. I certainly have determined that it's miles a incredible concept to be thoughtful of the alternative character's time. The actual chat does no longer should be prolonged. I try this frequently with colleague Peter Daisyme. Peter has worked throughout the united states of america from me for the last 4 years, but we've got got have been given had every day chats and supplied companies collectively. Take the time to choose up the cellular smartphone or Skype with that friend. It'll pass an extended an extended way to organising and building excellent connections.

10. Find commonplace interests.

It may be the identical sports activities sports team, tune, film, career, or immoderate activity. No recall how big or tiny, discovering a similar hobby is one of the best processes to enlarge a long-lasting friendship.

Eleven. Pay it in advance.

You must want to offer them matters due to the truth you want to. Not because you need to. If you apprehend someone who happens to be a exceptional internet fashion style clothier and you've got some other pal who desires a dressmaker, then why not introduce them to each other? Did you run upon an bizarre shot glass that might wholesome your pal's series? Could you easily collect it?

12. Don't wait to be asked for aid.

If that a coworker, friend, or member of the family desires some shape of useful resource, then step in and provide your assist in advance than they ask. For example, in case you recognize that they are moving and you have the time, you can volunteer to assist, in spite of the reality that your frame will hate it the next day.

Thirteen. Learn to accept as true with humans.

Even if you have been harmed thru a person in the beyond, either professionally or emotionally, you need to learn how to keep in mind once more. As George P.H. So honestly locations it "ALL relationships – own family, commercial enterprise corporation, platonic – need don't forget."

14. Be clear about what you desire.

None people revel in feeling upset. But, did you ever pause and realise that perhaps you did not have your desires addressed due to the fact you did not give an explanation for what you desired? Even even though it sounds hard, continually be honest about what you need or need.

15. Understand what is definitely being requested.

Here's each other little little bit of know-how from Steve Boyer. He believes that "humans will continuously ask considered one of a kind questions than the simplest they truly need to have replied." For example, "people normally inquire the way to be greater a success whilst all they certainly need is to acquire a boom or promoting." In different terms, there's a extra question prepared to be addressed inside the lower returned of that specific question.

Sixteen. Respond straight away.

While you do not have get entry to in your telephone or computer 24/7, there may be a large threat that you will at a while sooner than later. If a person emails or texts you a question or inquiry, solution them ASAP. Wouldn't you instead be diagnosed due to the fact the quick responder than the simplest who in no way gets once more?

17. Set calendar reminders.

We're all busy bees, so it is clean to lose contact with buddies, coworkers, own family individuals, and pals. To prevent any difficulty, hire a difficult and rapid-up calendar reminder so that you may set up a time to touch base with the people in life.

18. Identify and keep away from interpersonal problems.

Numerous attributes might be destructive to a relationship. The Counseling Center on the University of Texas lists the following:

Having unreasonable expectations of oneself, the opportunity character, or the connection in trendy.

Coming too near too quickly, bodily or mentally.

Being pessimistic about self, the connection, or life.

Being a rescuer, a martyr, a savior, or a "ideal" person.

Trying to regulate the opportunity individual to suit your wishes.

Being overly self-targeted, judgemental, or usually "accurate".

Stockpiling powerful sentiments - wrath, affliction, depression, neediness - after which pouring they all out immediately.

Expecting the other man or woman to be a mind reader, a fixer, or usually a rock of stability for you.

If you find any of those conduct in your self, bear in thoughts trying to modify them. You may also even need to gather assist from a person you take delivery of as real with so that you can forestall the selection from going any in addition.

19. Don't be judgemental.

Just due to the fact a person acts a specific manner, behaves in ways we might not allow ourselves to, or has opportunity beliefs, it does no longer imply that they're below you, or a good deal much less than you. Instead of casting judgment, why now not ask them inquiries to discover why they have got positive beliefs and pastimes. Besides learning a few aspect new, you may apprehend which you're no longer so precise ultimately.

20. Pick your venues and sports activities intelligently.

Heading out to the pub to fulfill new buddies appears wonderful in principle, possibly. But, you may most in reality gather bar buddies. Are they the parents you may certainly depend on? While there's not some component incorrect with having buddies, try to spend time in locations where there may be humans with comparable pursuits. If you want reading, for instance, then why no longer be part of a e-book membership?

21. Be affected man or woman.

Building and sustaining a connection takes time. During that period, you're going to require endurance to assist cope with the everyday problems of life. If you do not have the staying strength to cope with life's tiny aggravations, then how will you need to have a sustainable relationship?

22. Make eye contact.

Research has lengthy tested that "folks that make eye contact are visible as more, "likable and smooth." Dr. Atsushi Senju tells the New York Times, "A fuller style of communique is possible right away after beginning eye touch."

23. Don't murmur.

Communication is a big detail of relationships. So, why may additionally want to you need to make talks difficult or doubtful due to the truth you cannot be understood? In case you have been no longer conscious, muttering is also a "signal of hid displeasure, resentment, disdain, or grief."

24. Laugh.

In case you have been not aware, guffawing is enormously infectious. Besides being superb on your well-known fitness, it may additionally "beautify our relationships by means of way of activating happy sensations and growing an emotional connection." Also, take a threat to chuckle at your self on occasion.

25. Let it pass.

Pick your fights cautiously. Even if you disagree with someone or sense the impulse to tell them "I knowledgeable you so," it's miles maximum essential to move on and permit it circulate. No one wants to pay hobby a lecture.

Chapter 11: The Most Effective Method To Start A Conversation

1. Get a few records approximately the situation

The most honest method for starting a communicate is to attract motivation from your environmental elements

Instances of normal activities wherein you have to start up a communicate:

•At the lunch table with an bizarre man or woman from every one-of-a-kind artwork branch or elegance.

•Remaining with others inside the passage trusting that elegance will begin.

•Sitting close to one greater voyager on a train or plane.

•Try now not to pose direct inquiries in normal life

•At get-together

As we mentioned formerly, the same old is that outsiders introduce themselves to every other.

In normal lifestyles, as an alternative, you could't be so instant.

Pose a sincere inquiry about the situation in place of the following person.

To slide right right into a dialogue, we're able to pose an inquiry approximately the situation we're in.

That gives us the motivation to start speaking, and it's no longer excessively proper away.

It assists with asking some aspect that you now have on the leading edge of your mind.

In any case, if you don't, you may incorporate your environmental factors or the state of affairs for motivation.

An instance of an ordinary communicate from the week before...

Last week I wound up close to every body on the train.

I'd been thinking of whether or not or not or no longer they served snacks equipped.

It modified right right into a characteristic icebreaker because it have grow to be at that point at the forefront of my mind and related straightforwardly to my environmental factors.

I asked her,

"Excuse me, do you've got were given any idea whether or not they serve snacks right proper right here?"

She responded with some thing like,

"Gee. Better recollect it, they want to!"

It grow to be regular for me to ask a next inquiry:

"Great, I not noted breakfast these days." (Theparents grinned)

Me: "Do you are taking this educate often?"

We want to go through some everyday stresses over beginning a talk, and in a while, i'll communicate follow-up questions.

2. Realize which you don't want to be clever

You don't ought to pose a profound or widespread inquiry.

What you ask isn't vital. You don't want to try to appear like novel or savvy to your most memorable association.

The great icebreakers are commonly fundamental.

Posing an inquiry is a way for flagging which you're cordial and open to social connection.

Casual dialogue is regularly normal, and those are suitable with that.

Casual banter is simplest a get-prepared for a considerably charming communicate.

Three. Check out on the heading in their toes and look

At the point whilst you recognize what to search for, you can tell from any individual's non-verbal verbal exchange whether or not or not they need to talk with you.

It's normally predicted to actually get a quick "positive" or "no" reply on your maximum memorable inquiry.

It doesn't endorse that individuals might alternatively no longer communicate with you, truly that you want to surrender them multiple moments to exchange to "social mode."

In any case, within the occasion that they just provide short responses on your next inquiries, it's usually clever to say "Much obliged" or "Decent speakme with you" and hold.

Check out the course in their feet and the bearing of their appearance.

If they turn away from you a great deal or factor their toes from you, it's usually expected a respectable signal that they need to cease the dialogue.

You can also want to have bunches of captivating things to talk about, however the distinctive character in all likelihood acquired't be in that body of thoughts for social connection.

It doesn't imply you've completed a few element incorrect, so make the effort no longer to and through using taking it.

Ensure your non-verbal conversation is cordial and open

Your non-verbal verbal exchange needs to fit your phrases;

It should flag which you are unfastened, reliable, and satisfied to talk.

Recollect to:

•Keep in touch.

Try not to get carried away, otherwise you'll seem like scary or unpleasant.

•Stand together together with your toes shoulder-width separated.

Try not to shake or affect because of the fact these trends motive you to appear worried.

•Stand or sit down down down upright, however, don't solidify your again.

•Push your chest out marginally and preserve your head up.

Great stance indicators truth.

•Utilize a certifiable grin.

At the component whilst we grin commonly, our eyes wrinkle mainly on the corners. You can rehearse this in a replicate so it comes correctly to you sooner or later of discussions.

Four. Ask for take a look at-up inquiries

To flag that we're keen on speaking with any man or woman, we're capable of ask observe-up inquiries.

In the version with the train, I inquired:

"Do you're taking this train often?"

That is a clean improvement regarding whether or not or now not or now not there have been snacks open and organized.

As in opposition to posing a development of popular inquiries like,

"Where are you from?"

"How could probable you realize people proper right here?" And

"What do you do?"

You can make use of observe-up questions to dig similarly.

For example:

You might also want to inquire,

"Where are you from?"

Determined by means of manner of way of,

"How may additionally want to or now not it is growing up there?"

And a quick time later,

"What do you miss the maximum about it?"

Diving into a topic like this in preference to posing shallow inquiries will in large make the talk critically fascinating.

Five. Blend posing inquiries with sharing approximately yourself

Step-by way of way of-step commands to preserve a communicate you start exciting and changed making use of the IFR approach

We might probable as a substitute now not pose such many inquiries in succession or cross on and on about ourselves.

So how would possibly you song down the equilibrium?

Utilize the IFR approach.

Ask: Pose a actual inquiry

Follow up: Ask a subsequent inquiry

Relate: Offer a smidgen approximately your self that connects with what they said

You can begin the circle once more with the beneficial aid of posing some other earnest inquiry (Ask).

A few days inside the past I changed into speakme with everybody who ended up being a film manufacturer.

This is how the communique went:

Ask:

Me: What sort of narratives do you do?

She: At the winning 2nd, I'm doing a movie on bodegas in New York City.

Follow up:

Me: Gracious, exciting. What's your movement item up thus far?

She: That nearly all bodegas appear to have tom cats!

Relate:

Me: Ha-ha, that's what i've seen. The one close to in which I live has a feline who usually sits on the counter.

And in a while, I ask (IFR rehash):

Me: Are you a pussycat individual?

It would be brilliant in case you made the communicate bypass this way and that.

They communicate a smidgen approximately themselves, we talk ourselves, then allow them to talk all all once more, consequently on.

6. Utilize inquiries with out a right or incorrect answer

A real inquiry is an inquiry that requires extra than a "Yes" or "No" consequently.

By the use of actual inquiries, humans frequently sense propelled to provide a greater prolonged reaction.

Instances of near-completed questions:

"Did you need university?

"What's your art work name?

"Is it stable to mention that you may break out this yr?

Instances of inquiries with out a proper or incorrect answer:

"How was school for you?

"What shape of art work do you do?

"What may your first-rate tour be like?

Notwithstanding, this doesn't endorse that each one close completed questions are horrible.

For instance, at the off risk that you begin a dialogue in everyday lifestyles, an inquiry with out a proper or incorrect answer can revel in excessively sudden, even as a close-by completed question is greater normal.

Chapter 12: The Most Effective Method To Start A Conversation(Contd.)

7. Realize that tone is a better priority than terms

The impact you are making on others is based halfway upon what you're pronouncing, but it basically in reality is predicated on the way you say it.

Many human beings middle masses round what to specific in vicinity of their conveyance.

You want to talk in a nicely-disposed and loosened-up manner of speakme.

On the off chance that you do, you don't want to strain over the correct terms you use.

You needn't trouble with it to BE sure to sound well-disposed and unfastened.

I used to rehearse by means of way of talking with myself in the reflect, and I propose that you do likewise.

Note that the models in this guide aren't "contents" or "enchantment terms."

Use languages that feels everyday to you.

Instances of a way to begin a talk in regular life:

As in opposition to manufacturing questions, you may get a few data about topics which is probably honestly charming or if no longer something else applicable to the scenario (as I did on that train).

Try now not to stress over posing clean inquiries.

On the off risk which you sound nicely-disposed and unfastened, the inquiries will seem normal.

While sitting near someone on a teach or plane:

You: "Do you've got any idea a manner to make the seats lean decrease returned?" (Question about the condition)

They: "You want to press the button to as a minimum one problem."

You: "Much obliged! Are you furthermore going to Denver?" (Shut take a look at-down query)

They: "Indeed, i'm! I will go to my loved ones."

You: "Pleasant, me as well. I haven't been home in a half three hundred and sixty five days.

"Where do you stay now?" (Sharing approximately yourself and asking an open ensuing request)

While associating for the duration of noon with a person from one more office at work:

You: "What shape of fish is that?" (Question approximately the circumstance)

They: "I don't comprehend in truth."

You: "I'm no fish master both, ha-ha. However, it appears outstanding.

"What place of business do you figure in?"

(They make experience of wherein they art work)

You: "Okay, super, I artwork at (receives a control on).

"How have to you want it around there?" (Sharing some factor vital to you and asking an open next inquiry)

Holding up with every other character inside the passageway for class to start:

You: "Is this the fabric technology auditorium?" (Question about the condition)

They: "Definitely."

You: "Amazing.

"What is your opinion about the take a look at?" (Open subsequent inquiry)

They: "I don't forget it'll workout consultation actually.

I felt like I were given a contend with at the cloth better yesterday once I went through it all yet again."

You: "Better receive as proper with it, same proper proper right here, despite the truth that I lacked the possibility and electricity of mind to have a have a examine the ultimate factor.

"Why you picked this direction?" (Sharing a few issue critical to you and asking an open subsequent inquiry)

Eight. Offer a notable remark

Utilize the Positive Comments method to with out problem start a speak with any person you've expressed Howdy to previously.

This is my skip-to approach with human beings i've certainly had quick communications with previously, just like a "Hello there" or a "How are you?"

Since you recognize each other a tad, you could be specifically greater honest than you can accompany popular outsiders.

Instances of activities in which you may employ this approach:

•While sitting close to all people you scarcely apprehend at a accomplice's supper.

•At the factor at the same time as you want to cope with all and sundry from some one of a kind splendor with who you've currently traded gestures inside the hall.

•At the point on the same time as you want to speak with the barista at the bistro in that you get your morning espresso every day.

In those situations, I offer a effective observation about a few factor inside the weather.

Instances of brilliant feedback:

"The salmon appears tasty!"

"This spot seems wonderful considering the reality that they redesigned it!"

"It smells remarkable in right here! I love the scent of newly cooked espresso."

(I don't offer specific feedback about them, e.G., "I like your get dressed," considering that this type of remark can revel in excessively personal on the off chance which you are in truth colleagues.)

At the thing even as you particular some uplifting notion, you'll placed on a display of being extra cordial.

All things taken into consideration, they don't have any acquaintance with you however, so their initial feeling of you'll be based on the preliminary no longer many words they pay interest.

You can now retain with the dialogue.

You have to likewise make use of a detail of those suggestions to move the speak along.

9. Utilize your 5 detects

It will in well-known be greater earnestly than anticipated to sincerely suspect in nice activities, and at instances it's difficult to concoct something to say regarding our environmental elements.

The five detects sporting activities can assist.

By tuning into your faculties and seeing what's happening round you, you could get the motivation you really need to start a communicate with each person.

It likewise is going approximately as an putting in place exercising that lessens your tension.

Rather than zeroing in in your true fears, you're surely present and residing at the time.

Utilize every taken into consideration one in each of your 5 schools to appearance topics in your modern-day scenario.

Check whether or not or no longer or now not there are things in your room which you is probably capable:

See

Hear

Feel

Taste

Smell

Have you tracked down five matters? Amazing!

Could you at any factor pick out a pair of things and praise them?

Or however, in the occasion which you want a actual take a look at, must you at any factor track down some factor high-quality to mention concerning every of the 5?

You can employ this technique at anything thing you want to start a dialogue.

This is the very detail I concocted after I did this hobby.

They are real instances of accurate inquiries to begin a communicate:

"I like indoor plant life. It makes the room hundreds more great."

"That is a thoughts-boggling plan for a kitchen."

"You can see truely far flung from here."

"I love the espresso scent."

"I hold considering whether or not or now not the coffee tastes top notch as it encourages me, or however at the off hazard that I in reality like the taste of the real espresso".

"I discover it not possible to withstand whilst the nights get a bit less warm."

However, David, you may be wondering, the ones are really negligible motives!

What we're doing proper right here is motioning inside the route of human beings,

"I'm not a hazard, and I'm available to make a communicate inside the event that you are."

There's no need to reputation on what you are saying - it's approximately what you carry.